"Kreger gives an incredible amount of information, yet meets the needs of many types of readers. The anecdotes are memorable, the tasks are engaging, and the structure allows people to read it on an intellectual or emotional level. Most importantly, she has provided a great bridge between the high-level, abstract BPD theories and research and the realities of everyday life."

—Patricia Davis, family member of a person with BPD

"The workbook is absolutely extraordinary. It's a masterpiece and one of a kind. I couldn't put it down. The Action Steps are right on target. Like *Stop Walking on Eggshells*, this book is another work of art."

—Rita Closson, M.A.

P9-CNH-943

THE
Stop Walking on Eggshells
WORKBOOK

PRACTICAL STRATEGIES

FOR LIVING WITH

SOMEONE WHO HAS

BORDERLINE

PERSONALITY DISORDER

RANDI KREGER

WITH JAMES PAUL SHIRLEY, L.M.S.W.

NEW HARBINGER PUBLICATIONS, INC.

Publisher's Note

This publication is designed to provide accurate and authoritative information in regard to the subject matter covered. It is sold with the understanding that the publisher is not engaged in rendering psychological, financial, legal, or other professional services. If expert assistance or counseling is needed, the services of a competent professional should be sought.

Distributed in the U.S.A. by Publishers Group West; in Canada by Raincoast Books; in Great Britain by Airlift Book Company, Ltd.; in South Africa by Real Books, Ltd.; in Australia by Boobook; and in New Zealand by Tandem Press.

Lyrics from "This Too Will Pass" written by Carrie Newcomer. Published by CARRIE NEWCOMER MUSIC/Administered by BUG. All rights reserved. Used by permission.
Quotes from *I'm Not Supposed to Be Here* by Rachel Reiland are reprinted with her permission. Published by Eggshells Press, 2002.
Quotes and recommendations from Teresa Whitehurst are printed with her permission.
Quotes from Helen S. are printed with her permission.
Quotes from Shannon Mike are printed with her permission.
Quotes from "Non-guy" are used with his permission.

Copyright © 2002 by Randi Kreger
New Harbinger Publications, Inc.
5674 Shattuck Avenue
Oakland, CA 94609

Cover design by Amy Shoup
Edited by Brady Kahn
Text design by Tracy Powell-Carlson

ISBN 1-57224-271-X Paperback

All Rights Reserved
Printed in the United States of America
New Harbinger Publications' Web site address: www.newharbinger.com

04   03   02

10   9   8   7   6   5   4   3   2   1

First printing

This book is dedicated to my husband, Robert L. Burko, a man who says he does not believe in unconditional love but gives it nevertheless. His love, acceptance, and willingness to support me and my BPD work over these past years have made this workbook possible and enriched the lives of thousands of people he will never know. Thank you.

Hold tight, hold hands with me
All is trouble just as far as you can see
So here we are and here we stand
So we'll stare it down just to prove that we can
And ride it out to the last
It's true, this too will pass.

Small comfort when it goes so deep
And you roll at night in fitful sleep
I'll tell you what I know
As sure as trouble comes
Yah, trouble will go
I'll say it though you didn't ask
It's true, this too will pass.

So lay it down, lay it down right here.
All your sorrows, all your troubles and your fears.

I can't tell you how it goes this far
Or explain why it gets so damn hard
Or there are times that shine like jewels
And will be all the brighter for what you've been through
So hold these times tightly clasped
It's true, this too will pass.

So out of the darkest place
And the hardest times that you've ever had to face
We're more tender than some would believe
And we still find it hard to ask for what we need
But don't give up too fast
It's true, this too will pass
It's true, this too will pass.

—Carrie Newcomer, "This Too Will Pass"

Contents

Part 1
From Confusion to Clarity: Understanding BPD

Foreword

In addition to directly helping friends and family members of people with Borderline Personality Disorder (BPD), this workbook offers mental health professionals a hopeful new approach for their clients who are in relationships with borderlines. Just as Al-Anon can be the practitioner's best friend in dealing with clients affected indirectly by alcoholism, *Stop Walking on Eggshells* (Mason and Kreger 1998) and this companion workbook, along with online support groups, can be the beginning of a community of support for people affected indirectly by BPD.

Today, BPD treatment has many of the same problems that faced addictions treatment in the early 1970s. At that time society tended to view addiction as a failure of personal morality as well as a deeply shameful personal problem. While most mental health practitioners were not quite so moralistic, many were still pessimistic about addiction and considered it difficult to treat at best. Two practices changed these attitudes. First, clinicians became more willing to work with self-help groups as allies in the treatment process. Secondly, they began including family members as an integral part of the treatment process. Consequently, improvements began to occur as those in the field began to recognize the indirect effects of addiction—i.e., codependence—as a separate interpersonal component that helps feed the cycle of addiction and needs separate clinical attention.

The same principles that worked with addiction are now proving to work where BPD is concerned. The commonsense simplicity of Kreger's interpersonal approach works, where the older, more limited intra-psychic individual approaches have often failed. In my role as a therapeutic consultant on Kreger's Internet family of support groups called "Welcome to Oz," I have seen people get results when they apply the principles contained in this workbook. I have heard people who are trying hard to cope with friends, partners, or family members with

BPD repeatedly insist that these online support groups—supplemented with information in *Stop Walking on Eggshells* (*SWOE*), Kreger's earlier book—have helped them more quickly and effectively than counseling did. (Research conducted by Kreger and statistics professor Edith Cracchiolo [Cracchiolo and Kreger 1997] showed that 75 percent of the [then 250] members of Welcome to Oz had sought professional help for their problems dealing with their significant others.)

Increasingly, I am now hearing online support group participants say they wish their therapists had had the information in *SWOE*, or wish that their therapists had referred them to Kreger's Web site and Welcome to Oz support groups. The combination of pertinent information, together with interpersonal support, is working.

The goal of this workbook is to re-create some of the helpful experiences of reading *SWOE* and participating in an online support group. Using realistic scenarios based on compilations of real-life experiences, Kreger and I take the reader through a series of Action Steps designed to build knowledge and confidence in applying the principles described in *SWOE*. The result is not an academic description of Borderline Personality Disorder, but rather a guide to help you cope with the problem behavior BPD causes.

Hopefully, the long-term result of our work will be a growing community of people who speak a common language, who know some techniques for dealing with BPD, and who understand how to apply those techniques in real-life situations. If this workbook helps just one person take back control of his or her life, then we will have succeeded.

—James Paul Shirley, M.S.W.

Acknowledgments

Although I am listed as the "author" of this workbook, there is no shortage of people whose contributions made this work possible. First, a heartfelt thanks to the primary contributors to this workbook, including James Paul Shirley, M.S.W., who reviewed the book and wrote many of the Action Steps, and editor and writer Wynne Brown, who was instrumental in editing the draft and writing certain sections about borderline offspring. Additional contributors include Rachel Reiland, author of *I'm Not Supposed to Be Here: My Recovery from Borderline Personality Disorder* (2002); Kathy Winkler, my coauthor of *Hope for Parents: Helping Your Borderline Son or Daughter without Sacrificing Your Family or Yourself* (Winkler and Kreger 2000); and Kim Williams-Justesen, my coauthor of *Love and Loathing: Protecting Your Mental Health and Legal Rights When Your Partner Has Borderline Personality Disorder* (Kreger and Williams-Justesen 1999). Thank you all.

In cyberspace, a thank-you to all those who created and participated in our Welcome to Oz (WTO) Internet community of friends and family members of those with Borderline Personality Disorder. The feedback from WTO members was invaluable in making this publication as effective as possible. I am also grateful for the continuing guidance and assistance of Rita Closson, M.A., social psychologist and list patrol chief, as well as Edith, James, Eric, and Deborah. This workbook reflects the accomplishments of all the WTO facilitators and their friends, past and present, who have consistently reminded me that the destructiveness of borderline behavior can be tempered or even eliminated by using the techniques in *Stop Walking on Eggshells* and this workbook.

In the "real" world, special thanks to those who made this workbook possible: my *Stop Walking on Eggshells* coauthor Paul Mason, M.S., my husband Robert Burko, my guardian angel Edith Cracchiolo, and all the staff at New

Harbinger—especially Patrick Fanning (my mentor through this project). From the owners to the people who work in customer service, everyone has been enthusiastic, supportive, and flexible. Their decisions to print *Stop Walking on Eggshells* and this workbook have helped thousands of people reclaim their lives.

Keeping up with orders for *Stop Walking on Eggshells* and the booklets I publish is a sensitive, crucially important job. Merci beaucoup to Alan, Mary Jane, and the staff at PIP Printing for keeping the booklets quickly flowing even when checks get backlogged, and Nancy, Diane, and all the staff at Book Clearing House in New York for their high-caliber service and compassion to callers.

Mental health writers whose work especially inspired me include Jan Black and Greg Enns and their incredible book *Better Boundaries: Owning and Treasuring Your Own Life* (1997); self-help author Beverly Engel, primarily for her book *Loving Him without Losing You* (2000); Christine Ann Lawson, *Understanding the Borderline Mother: Helping Her Children Transcend the Intense, Unpredictable, and Volatile Relationship* (2000); and Susan Forward and Donna Frazier, especially their book *Emotional Blackmail: When the People in Your Life Use Fear, Obligation and Guilt to Manipulate You* (1997).

In addition to James Paul Shirley and Paul Mason, clinicians who graciously gave me their time for an interview for this workbook include George Smith, L.I.C.S.W., associate director of outpatient personality disorders service at McLean Hospital; and Teresa Whitehurst, Ph.D., clinical instructor at Harvard Medical School and director of the Cambridge Family Language Project.

Finally, thanks for the encouragement and validation of Mary, J.T., and a few others who kept reminding me that this work is important and that I need to keep going, no matter what. You all sustain me and make it all possible.

Introduction

I never set out to dedicate more than five years to researching and writing about how the behavior of those with Borderline Personality Disorder (BPD) affects family members. You don't choose some jobs, they choose you. Or as singer/songwriter Carrie Newcomer puts it in "Close Your Eyes," "How I got this job I'll never know, but when it calls, you can't refuse to go."

My involvement with BPD began as a personal quest. In the early 1990s, I learned that a person who had had a large influence on my life suffered from some of the traits of BPD. Since I had never heard of this disorder, I eagerly looked for information about how such distorted behavior affects loved ones. I discovered that few clinicians knew the answers—or, frankly, were even looking.

I found this extraordinary. Borderline Personality Disorder by definition negatively involves other people, according to the *Diagnostic and Statistical Manual of Mental Disorders* (*DSM-IV*) (APA 1994), the standard reference for the diagnosis and treatment of psychiatric illnesses. To others, people with BPD can appear to be emotionally or verbally abusive, manipulative, deceitful, invalidating, demanding, lacking in empathy, illogical, unfair, self-absorbed, and abusive to children. This is a result of their inner pain. But the effects can still be devastating. Why wasn't anyone studying this?

According to the *DSM-IV*, BPD affects 2 percent of the population, about 6 million people in North America. But that statistic is artificially low. When I give workshops to clinicians, about half of them say that they have learned to put the client's secondary diagnosis (common ones include depression, eating disorder, or substance abuse) on the client's chart. They do this for two reasons: one, some insurance companies refuse to pay for treatments for personality disorders. They consider them "incurable" despite medications and therapies that have been shown to improve BPD symptoms. Secondly, mental health practitioners want to protect BPD patients from the dreaded "Borderline Stigma"—its main symptom being a scarlet "B" carved in patients' foreheads by other practitioners who blame them for not getting better or choose not to treat people with this diagnosis. Therefore, I believe that 2 percent figure is a gross underestimate.

Assuming that each borderline individual (BP) affects three other people, BPD behavior impacts 30 million people. The price is enormous: high-conflict divorce, substance abuse, suicide, lost productivity, criminal activity, domestic violence, hospitalization, therapist burnout, and more. The total amount of money and productivity lost is unknown, but is probably in the millions of dollars.

But money is not my greatest concern. I do this work to help prevent abusive borderlines who refuse treatment from being abusive to children (who are at risk of becoming borderline themselves) and to empower partners who feel helpless to stop emotional, verbal, and even physical abuse. Even though borderlines usually do not intend to be abusive, their actions can be abusive. And verbal and emotional abuse is just as bad as physical abuse in terms of contributing to BPD. In other words, my mission is prevention, not treatment, of BPD.

When I realized that I couldn't depend on the mental health profession, the media (which mostly covers illnesses with celebrity spokespeople), or even public or private mental health organizations to provide support and information about the many different ways BPD affects the sufferer and the people around them, I decided to start an Internet support group and write a book (eventually called *Stop Walking on Eggshells*) with therapist Paul Mason, M.S.

Our hope was to validate the experiences of the millions of "nonborderlines," or non-BPs (partners, friends, or family member of a person with BP); increase awareness of all types of the disorder; and teach coping methods and healthier behaviors to family members and friends who experience BPD behavior as confusing, chaotic, or abusive. While Paul squeezed whatever he could out of the scientific studies, I started speaking with other people related to borderlines the only place I could find them: on the Internet and America Online.

In order to share stories, in December 1995 I started an Internet listserv support group with the technical help of a computer guru from the Netherlands. The Welcome to Oz list (the title refers to Dorothy's disorientation when she travels from Kansas to Oz) has blossomed into a family of groups, totaling 2,000 members.

Paul Mason and I used these Internet discussions as a blueprint for *Stop Walking on Eggshells* (*SWOE*), which New Harbinger published in July 1998. "The Little Book that Could" went on to sell 45,000 copies (as of this writing) and make Amazon.com's "Movers and Shakers" list several times. Not bad for a specialized book originally rejected by thirty publishers because the audience was "too narrow" and "no one ever heard of Borderline Personality Disorder."

Using the tools and information in *Stop Walking on Eggshells*, as well as their own insights and support gained from each other, readers and online support group participants began to take back control of their lives—even when their disordered family member or friend refused treatment or joint-relationship problem solving. The site and list helped spur others to develop their own sites and lists, creating a wellspring of information on the Internet about BPD.

I went on to found my own publishing company, Eggshells Press, and produce materials that *Stop Walking on Eggshells* could not address in detail for lack of space. These include *Love and Loathing: Protecting Your Mental Health and Legal Rights When Your Partner Has Borderline Personality Disorder* (Kreger and Wiliams-Justesen 1999); *Hope for Parents: Helping Your Borderline Son or Daughter without Sacrificing Your Family or Yourself* (Winkler and Kreger 2000); the three-set CD *You're My World: A Non-BP's Guide to Custody* (see appendix A); and *I'm Not Supposed to Be Here: My Recovery from Borderline Personality Disorder* (Reiland 2002).

Most authors have little contact with their readers. But because of the Internet support groups and several in-person gatherings, I was able to assess how well non-BPs were understanding and using the principles and techniques in *Stop Walking on Eggshells* (also known as *SWOE*). Over the years, dozens of list members told me that *SWOE* was so densely packed with information that they had to read it several times, highlighting important sections and making notes in the margins. Clearly, BP and non-BP interactions are so complex that people need assistance to apply the material in *SWOE* to their own lives.

For example, people wanted to know, "Why did the BP in my life do this?" "What should I have done in this situation?" and "What does this confusing behavior mean?" BPD is a complex disorder, and intellectual knowledge doesn't necessarily translate into personal enlightenment. Most importantly, it takes time and feedback for non-BPs to go through the stages of grief and the five stages of the BP/non-BP relationships detailed in *SWOE*.

Thus, the idea for this workbook was born. It is not based on scientific studies; they don't exist. It's not a scientific book about BPD; in fact, it's not about BPD. It's about how to live with someone who has the disorder and still feel in control of your own life. It's based on my own experiences with BPs and non-BPs, interviews with clinicians, and my work cofacilitating the Welcome to Oz lists for five years. In order to show you how BPD behavior works in real life, some of the exercises, or Action Steps, use portions of *I'm Not Supposed to Be Here*.

This workbook is also not a non-BP "bible" (as some people refer to *SWOE*) because too many variables exist to make the work complete. People with BPD act in a variety of ways—some 180 degrees differently—making the needs of family members and friends extremely different as well. The concerns of non-BPs also differ according to the type of relationship between BP and non-BP. Therefore, rather than try to make this workbook everything to everyone, I've decided to keep things as simple and universal as possible. For more specific information, you may wish to read *SWOE* and the material listed in the bibliography.

But if you want this workbook to really help you, you can't just read it. You need to do the Action Steps in the order presented, and practice the techniques. Ideally, you'll have already read *Stop Walking on Eggshells* or plan to do so at the same time you go through this workbook (although it's not required). If you can't find *SWOE* in your local bookstore or library, see appendix A for information on how to get this book.

I also recommend a visit to the New Harbinger Web site (www.NewHarbinger.com), which offers books and tapes about related issues, such as narcissistic parents, boundaries, anger, assertiveness, stress, anxiety, substance abuse, trauma, self-forgiveness, parenting, and other issues pertinent to readers. They also carry a self-help book for those who wish to overcome BPD called *The Angry Heart: Overcoming Borderline and Addictive Disorders* (Santoro and Cohen 1997).

One last significant bit of information. Many BPs are in a great deal of emotional anguish and are regular users of the mental health system. These BPs are well known to clinicians and some mental health organizations because they are low-functioning BPs who readily admit that they have problems. If you are reading this book, however, you are probably in a relationship with someone who has borderline traits but is in denial about it. *SWOE* readers and WTO members are almost always in relationships in which the person who has borderline traits not only refuses treatment but feels that any problems in the relationship are the other person's fault.

Most clinicians and BPD organizations I have come into contact with work with families where a diagnosis has been made, each person takes some responsibility, and family members sometimes work in treatment together. They are unfamiliar with the high-functioning, non-self-harming BPs, and one group even denies that they exist.

The difference between working with the non-BPs of low-functioning BPs who acknowledge they have a problem and the non-BPs of high-functioning ones who do not admit to having a problem is as different as working with alcoholics in denial and alcoholics in treatment or Alcoholics Anonymous. If the BP in your life is willing to work in treatment and try new ways of relating, wonderful! You're already halfway there. If not, be aware that this workbook will help you do what you need to do to take care of yourself and, most importantly, any children who are involved. I believe that while adults are capable of making their own decisions about relationships, minor children are not. The BP can be a powerful, fearsome force, and adults who understand what's going on are morally bound—I believe—to protect these children. Appendix C contains specific suggestions for safely removing yourself and any children who are involved from abusive situations.

I hope this workbook helps you better understand yourself and the BP in your life, and enables you to make the best decisions for yourself and any children who rely on your love, support, and protection.

Part 1

From Confusion to Clarity: Understanding BPD

Chapter 1

Walking on Eggshells: Does Someone in Your Life Have BPD Traits?

I feel like I've been forced to drink three shots, put through the spin cycle of a washing machine, and asked to play Pin the Tail on the Donkey. And if I don't put the tail in the right place, God help me.

—a member of the Welcome to Oz Internet
support list

You're probably reading this workbook because you suspect that someone in your life has Borderline Personality Disorder. Or perhaps the title struck a chord. It's possible that a friend or therapist recommended it, or that you've read *Stop Walking on Eggshells: Taking Your Life Back When Someone You Care About Has Borderline Personality Disorder,* by Paul Mason, M.S., and myself (1998).

Whatever the circumstances, it's likely that a current or past relationship is causing you pain. The person who is the source of this grief may be alive and part of your everyday life. Or he could be a long-deceased parent. You may not understand who or what is responsible for the distress, let alone what to do about it. You may not even be able to describe how it has affected you. But like the main character in *The Matrix,* you sense that something is wrong and has been for a long time.

Borderline Personality Disorder causes distress for both people who have the disorder and those who interact with them. Because of some combination of biological or environmental factors, people with BPD are in a great deal of pain. They may feel shame and self-loathing, and question who they really are. Their intense fear of abandonment and an alternating need for intimacy and separation often leads to unstable relationships. (I'll give a more complete definition in chapter 2.)

How Do You Feel Right Now?

Do you feel isolated, distrustful, and flawed? Do you live in fear of disagreements, unable to do anything but wait for the other shoe to drop—or fly across the room? Do you feel trapped and helpless, unable to leave or stay in an important but unhealthy relationship?

You may be one of 30 million people in the United States and Canada (millions more live overseas) who are "nonborderlines," or non-BPs, someone whose life is being affected by a person who has the traits of Borderline Personality Disorder. This disordered thinking and emotion has a name, a diagnosis. And now, with the help of this workbook and some other recommended resources, you can do something about it.

How This Workbook Can Help

Some brain disorders, like depression, most directly affect those who have it. Yes, other people cope with the fallout. But if you put a depressed woman on a tropical island, alone except for a fishing pole and some matches, you'd still have a depressed woman. A *hungry* depressed woman with a bad sunburn. The most important point for you to understand is that she is the one most affected.

But personality disorders are different. They affect both the people who have them, and by definition, their friends, family members, and anyone who comes in contact with them. If you put a man with borderline traits (a BP) on a deserted island, sneak a microphone underneath some shrubbery and spy on him with a

telescope, it will be difficult to observe crucial BPD traits such as identity disturbance, pattern of unstable interpersonal relationships, or frantic efforts to avoid
real or imagined abandonment. These traits simply won't show up unless he has
other people to interact with. As stated in the *Diagnostic and Statistical Manual of
Mental Disorders* (*DSM-IV*) (APA 1994), a guidebook to mental illness published by
the American Psychiatric Association, some traits of personality disorders require
another person to witness or take part in the interaction (or "the BPD Dance").

📖 *Action Step 1:*
Prioritizing Skills Taught in this Workbook

This workbook will teach you many skills, some of which I've listed below. Put a
"1" by the ones that are most important to you, a "2" by those that are of secondary concern, and a "3" by those that are of least concern. This workbook will:

_____ Help you tell whether or not someone in your life has BPD traits

_____ Explain how it has affected you and others, so you can try to undo the
damage

_____ Focus on how BPD behavior affects you so you can prevent negative
consequences

_____ Understand how people with BPD see the world and how that impacts your
life—and theirs

_____ Understand why BPs act in ways that confuse you, so you'll know how to
respond

_____ Explain how the brain processes emotions, so you can make better decisions

_____ Measure the true costs of this disorder, to motivate you to make changes

_____ Identify your reactions to BPD behavior, so you can respond more effectively

_____ Help you let the BP in your life take responsibility for his own behavior so he
can learn from it

_____ Help you take responsibility for your own behavior, which leads to a feeling
of control

_____ Explain how to exert more control in your life, so you actually "own it"

_____ Help prevent you from making the same mistakes again and again

_____ Show you how to minimize chaos and dangerous situations

_____ Help you discover and communicate your personal limits

_____ Help you communicate these limits with the BP in your life

_____ Help you find competent, qualified professional help

_____ Help you choose among the many options available to you

In this chapter, we will examine BPD from your perspective and show you how to start your own emotional first aid kit. In the next chapter, we'll look at the ways clinicians define Borderline Personality Disorder.

Intellectual, Emotional, and Personal Comprehension

Before you start the rest of this book, I'd like to explain how you will need to engage yourself on three levels—intellectual, emotional, and personal—to get the most out of this workbook.

The intellectual, emotional, and personal tracks are like three different journeys out of the Land of Oz of differing hardships and they reach somewhat different destinations. The people on each platform all want to get someplace else because their current circumstances are intolerable. But the amount of energy and emotion they put into the journey affects where they end up.

The Intellectual Track

People who read this workbook to further their intellectual understanding of BPD are like train travelers on a comfortable excursion out of the Emerald City. With no heavy suitcases and even terrain, the trip is not too taxing. In other words, understanding theories about BPD as if you were a psychology major is not effortless, but it's less threatening than letting yourself feel emotions that may have been buried for a long time. It's easier, but the payoff at the end is not as great. Rather than truly experiencing the journey along the way, you gaze at the scenery from behind the glass on the train. You may go through this workbook quickly instead of slowly working the Action Steps. So at the end of the "trip," you may find that your final destination isn't as different from your current situation as you had hoped. That's okay. Right now, do what feels comfortable. When you are ready to examine something emotionally (see the next level), you will know.

The Emotional Track

These travelers are carrying heavy suitcases full of guilt, sorrow, fear, denial, and other mixed emotions. When the train stops, they venture out to breathe the air in this new, cleaner environment. In other words, they may work the Action Steps and clarify their feelings about their situation, as well as understand it intellectually. But changing how they feel is not so easy. At the end of the journey, they can see their final destination—a place where they can detach from other people's problems but still care about them, and a place where someone else's pain doesn't become their own. But the gates to their new destination are locked, and the key doesn't quite fit. This stage is probably a necessary part of the trip. It takes time for intellectual understanding to sink down into that place in your body where you really and truly feel changed. Again, give it time and be kind to yourself.

The Personal Change Track

The personal change track is for those ready to not only do the Action Steps but to work hard to incorporate their new understanding into the way they feel and interact with the BP in their life. For example, it is one thing to understand that the BP's problems do not have to be a crisis for you. But it's more difficult to actually detach from the BP's problems and help the BP gain confidence so that she can solve some of her problems on her own.

Change is painful, but so is staying where you are. It will take time to really incorporate some of this advice into your own life. Even after you do, you may feel uncertain about this change because it is unfamiliar. You may have to grieve for what you've never had, sob your heart out for what you've lost, and come to terms with facts you cannot change. But your hard work will be rewarded. At the end of the journey, you will gain the key to a new life that you control. Your days will not be full of chaos, the pain of others, or a useless obsession with trying to change someone else. You will be in a place where you choose your own destiny and no longer *react*, but *act* in your own best interest.

Even if this place seems far off, I promise you can get there. Not all at once, perhaps. The train may go very slowly. But you can make it. Take it easy and don't expect perfection. Give yourself room to make mistakes, and that goes for the other stages as well. I promise the destination is worth the trip.

Your Role in the BPD Dance

If we use dance as a metaphor for BPD behavior, in this book *I've assumed your borderline loved one can't or won't change the way he or she dances.* For the purposes of this book, Scrooge does not buy Tiny Tim a turkey, the bigot doesn't become the leader of the local civil rights movement, and the thief doesn't decide to donate his bounty to the children's orphanage. People with BPD do recover, but this workbook is for non-BPs who care about someone who doesn't believe he or she has anything to recover *from*.

Once you truly accept this (yes, I know it's easier said than done), you can come to terms with the fact that you can only change yourself. This will enable you to feel less trapped and open your eyes to the variety of options before you.

For example, you can change the way you look at the BP's behavior, you can set limits that have consequences, you can end the "blame game," or you can sell everything and move to Hawaii. If you have children, your first duty should be to protect them. After that, the world is open to you.

This workbook will help you connect your logic and emotions and teach you how to:

* Step back to see the "dance" (interaction) for what it really is. This requires you to objectively observe behavior (yours and theirs) and identify unhealthy patterns.

* Help you recognize how the BP is "leading" the dance and how you're following as best you can, backwards. In your case, you can *act* as well as *react*.

* Teach you how to initiate your own healthier steps—in other words, start acting in your own best interest and the best interest of your family instead of just tolerating circumstances beyond your control. As an adult, you can create the circumstances that are best for you and your family.

* Once you learn these new "steps," you can model them for others who need help, including the person with BPD and other members of your family (including children).

You Can *Improve Your Situation by Changing Yourself*

Right now, you probably believe that the BP in your life must change for things to improve. It's especially galling to be told *you* have to be the one to change if the BP in your life is your thirteen-year-old child. So it's crucial that you understand the difference between accepting "blame" and making changes on your own.

If you really had the power to change the behavior of others, you could be using your abilities to enable world peace. At the very least, you could charge retailers $300 an hour to tell them how to get people to clamor for their products. But you probably find it difficult enough to change *yourself*, even when you want to. So what is the chance of someone changing when they don't want to? About zero. Perhaps negative ten. *People change when the pain they're in is worse than the fear of the unknown.* The more you spare the BP from reaping the natural consequences of his behavior, the less likely it is that he will change. *That is your power: the ability to take control of your own life, make the best choices for yourself, and let the BP face the consequences of his own actions.*

Changing Doesn't Mean You're "Wrong"

Needing to change yourself doesn't mean that you're not okay the way you are. Rather, here it means that because someone you care about has a personality disorder, you are more psychologically capable of modifying your behavior to improve the relationship, if that is your goal. Let's use an analogy. What would you do if the person you care about had a broken arm? You'd have to settle for making dinner (or eating out) for a while. Think of BPD as an extended broken arm that the BP can either ignore or choose to treat. This fact *empowers you.* It means that you can choose to:

* Feel less manipulated

* Feel less trapped

* Better understand the person in your life with BPD

* Serve as a good role model for other vulnerable people (especially children)

However, you're not obliged to change you fundamental values and let the BP or anyone else walk all over you. You might choose to clean house and cook for a month for a family member who is ill. But if the family member refused to do what the doctor ordered to improve her health, your patience would probably wear thin.

In the same way, the BP in your life didn't ask to have the disorder. You can take a leap of faith and act in ways that make her more comfortable. But you don't have to spend your life walking on eggshells if she refuses to acknowledge the problem and seek help.

The First Steps of the Journey

Your first task is to determine whether or not one or more people in your life have traits of Borderline Personality Disorder. Although it's never easy accepting that a loved one has a brain disorder (a personality disorder is a brain disorder because it has medical causes as well as environmental influences), most people feel enormously relieved when they learn there is a name for their experiences and they're not going crazy. This applies to both BPs and those who are affected by their behavior. If you have a parent with BPD, you may have selected a partner with BPD. And if you selected a partner with BPD, chances are that any children you have are learning to incorporate BPD coping skills into their repertoire.

As you use this workbook, there will be some Action Steps that are open-ended questions. Please buy a notebook or blank book, or use a computer to respond to these questions. If you would like something more structured with the questions in it and additional tips for non-BPs, you can purchase the *Stop Walking on Eggshells Action Step Journal* (see appendix A). When the Action Step should be recorded in your journal, you'll see a 📖 symbol.

📖 *Action Step 2:*
Does Someone in Your Life Have BPD Traits?

Most psychological tests that are used to determine if someone has BPD are oriented toward the client or patient. The following questions, which originally appeared in *SWOE* (Mason and Kreger 1998) which publisher McGraw-Hill is using in three of its textbooks, are better suited for friends and family members to determine if someone in their life has BPD. Since you cannot know how the BP feels, using your own feelings as a gauge has proven to be a better indicator of whether or not someone in your life has BPD traits. (However, it is not scientific, just an indicator.) Please answer the following questions, putting a check mark by the words that best describes the extent of each problem.

1. Do you find yourself hiding negative thoughts or feelings because it's easier than dealing with the other person's overreactions or because talking about problems simply makes them worse?

_____ Not a problem

_____ Sometimes a problem

_____ A problem half of the time

_____ A frequent concern

_____ An ongoing problem of great concern

2. After you try to explain yourself to the other person, does she use your own words and contort them to prove her own point (usually that you are "bad" or doing something wrong)? Does this person blame you for all the problems in her life (and your relationship) and refuse to acknowledge that her own actions cause problems for other people and herself?

_____ Not a problem

_____ Sometimes a problem

_____ A problem half of the time

_____ A frequent concern

_____ An ongoing problem of great concern

3. Is his temper so unpredictable that you're constantly on your toes, adrenaline pumping, waiting for the next verbal attack? When you try to calm him down, does it only make him angrier? Is it difficult to enjoy the good times because you've been sucked in too often and you've learned to never let your guard down?

_____ Not a problem

____ Sometimes a problem

____ A problem half of the time

____ A frequent concern

____ An ongoing problem of great concern

4. Do you feel as if the other person sees you as either all good or all bad, with nothing in between? Is there sometimes no rational reason for the switch? When you come home from work each day, do you wonder who will greet you at the door: the person who basks in your love or the petty tyrant whose energy supply seems to come from intense, violent, and irrational rages? Does no one believe you when you explain that this is going on?

____ Not a problem

____ Sometimes a problem

____ A problem half of the time

____ A frequent concern

____ An ongoing problem of great concern

5. Do you feel manipulated, controlled, or even lied to sometimes? Does this person attempt to get what they want by making you responsible for their feelings (e.g., "If you don't let me go to the rock concert, I swear I'll hate you for the rest of my life." Or, "Only an ungrateful and selfish daughter would rather stay at school for Christmas instead of coming home.")

____ Not a problem

____ Sometimes a problem

____ A problem half of the time

____ A frequent concern

____ An ongoing problem of great concern

6. Does this person seem to demand constant attention? Is everything always about her—say, even your personal medical decisions? For example, can your borderline sister manage being at a birthday party when the focus is on someone else? Or will she push through people's boundaries and ignore good manners by creating a scene that will bring the attention back to her?

____ Not a problem

____ Sometimes a problem

____ A problem half of the time

____ A frequent concern

_____ An ongoing problem of great concern

7. Are you afraid to ask for things in the relationship because you will be told that you're selfish and demanding? Does this person imply, explicitly declare, or show by example that your needs are not as important as his are?

_____ Not a problem

_____ Sometimes a problem

_____ A problem half of the time

_____ A frequent concern

_____ An ongoing problem of great concern

8. Does this person continually contradict your needs and opinions so he can be the voice of authority? Do you feel that his expectations of you are constantly changing so you can never do anything right?

_____ Not a problem

_____ Sometimes a problem

_____ A problem half of the time

_____ A frequent concern

_____ An ongoing problem of great concern

9. Are you accused of doing things you never did and saying things you never said? Do you feel misunderstood, and when you try to explain, do you find that the other person doesn't believe you?

_____ Not a problem

_____ Sometimes a problem

_____ A problem half of the time

_____ A frequent concern

_____ An ongoing problem of great concern

10. Do other people remark that this other person is verbally and emotionally abusive or encourage you to leave the relationship? If and when you try to leave, does the other person attempt to prevent you from departing by trying to convince you that no one else loves you more or could put up with someone like you?

_____ Not a problem

_____ Sometimes a problem

____ A problem half of the time

____ A frequent concern

____ An ongoing problem of great concern

11. Do you have a hard time planning social engagements, vacations, and other activities because the other person's moodiness, impulsiveness, or unpredictability may destroy your plans at the last minute? Do you make excuses for her behavior to convince others (and yourself) that this is okay?

____ Not a problem

____ Sometimes a problem

____ A problem half of the time

____ A frequent concern

____ An ongoing problem of great concern

12. Right now, are you thinking, "I had no idea that anyone else was going through this"?

____ Yes

____ No

Now, score your answers for the first eleven questions in this way:

* Not a problem = 0

* Sometimes a problem = 1

* A problem half the time = 2

* A frequent concern = 3

* An ongoing problem of great concern = 4

For the last question, give a "Yes" 3 points and a "No" 0 points. Now compare your total figure with the corresponding number below:

* A score of about 20 indicates that someone in your life probably has BPD traits.

* A score of 11–20 indicates a relationship with a "borderline" borderline: someone who may have BPD leanings but who can keep them somewhat in check.

* A score of 11 or below probably means that either the person in your life doesn't have BPD or is the "quiet, acting-in" type of BP and focuses his problems inwardly (by self-mutilation and attempting suicide) rather than outwardly toward you.

📖 *Action Step 3:*
Examples from Your Own Life

Now, take a look at the questions you answered with a 2 ("a problem half the time"), a 3 ("a frequent concern"), or a 4 ("an ongoing problem of great concern"). Jot down some examples from your own life in your notebook. You don't have to write the entire story, just enough to jog your memory. I've included examples below to help you. As with all the examples in this book, the stories are based on those shared on the Internet support groups, though I have changed many details to conceal their identities.

1. Do you find yourself hiding negative thoughts or feelings because it's easier than dealing with the other person's overreactions, or because talking about problems simply makes them worse?

   Gail's response: *During the years I've learned not to contradict my mother when she's in one of her moods—especially when she's been drinking, too. She gets argumentative over nothing and tries to pound it into my head. I don't say anything because whatever I say will be wrong. If she asks me a question, I just say, "I don't know." Even though I'm thirty-three, I remember the day I discovered I could just say "I don't know" (I was only eleven) and sometimes that worked to shut her up. At the time, I thought all mothers acted that way.*

2. After you try to explain yourself to the other person, does she use your own words and contort them to prove her own point (usually that you are "bad" or doing something wrong)? Does this person blame you for all the problems in her life (and your relationship) and refuse to acknowledge that her own actions cause problems for other people and herself?

   Rochelle's response: *I drove out to Georgia to visit my sister-in-law, nieces, and BP brother. It's been a long time since I've seen him because of his BP behavior, but since I was going in that direction I figured I might as well stop by. So when I brought up the fact that we hadn't spoken in a long time, he started yelling at me that I never cared about him, that our parents loved me more—which I don't think is true, except that he caused them a lot of grief. He kept going on and I couldn't go anywhere because we were in the car. And he's saying that we all expected him to be a doctor and not a medical technologist. Then out of nowhere he started accusing me of telling the photographer at my wedding (in 1994!) not to take pictures of him. Huh?*

3. Is his temper so unpredictable that you're constantly on your toes, adrenaline pumping, waiting for the next verbal attack? When you try to calm him down, does it only make him angrier? Is it difficult to enjoy the good times because you've learned not to let down your guard?

Bill's response: *Our son is sixteen, so sometimes it's hard to see where typical BPD behavior and typical teen behavior start and stop. Since he won't go to therapy, it probably doesn't matter. We live our lives in fear. We sleep in our clothes with our car keys under the pillow in case we need to get out of the house ASAP because of his physical threats. Every time the phone rings late at night, we expect it to be the hospital. When the door rings unexpectedly, our automatic thought is, "He's overdosed, gotten in a car wreck, shoplifted, whatever—and it's the police."*

His therapy has cost us thousands of dollars—money we could have used to send our daughter to college. We have no idea how she has been affected by this and, frankly, we're afraid to dig deep. He is involved in some illegal activities, and he laughs at our attempts to punish him. What are we supposed to do, lock him in his room? When he threatened us with bodily harm, we finally got him hospitalized. But he quickly learned the "game" and gave them the answers he knew they wanted. We are counting the days until he is eighteen and we are no longer legally responsible for his actions. We love him, but we've learned that love is not enough.

4. Do you feel like the person you care about sees you as either all good or all bad, with nothing in between? Is there sometimes no rational reason for the switch? When you come home from work each day, do you wonder who will greet you at the door: the person who basks in your love or the petty tyrant whose energy supply seems to come from intense, violent, and irrational rages? Does no one believe you when you explain that this is going on?

Susan's response: *My partner and I have a small public relations agency. We were so excited when we landed a major project for a mortgage insurance agency—promoting an incentive program for the loan processors who often make the decision as to which MI company to use. We knew we needed help, so we asked my ad agency friend Rob if he would help us out on a freelance, hourly basis. I had known Rob for about a year after we met at a neighborhood watch meeting. We began to meet every Sunday morning for coffee at a nearby café. Rob, Joan, and I generated a lot of ideas and ended up with an incentive program that the client really loved.*

The trouble began when Joan and I as owners of the agency flew down to make the presentation. Rob felt slighted and complained loudly, claiming that we should have paid to fly him, too. Then he wanted an office and computer. It seemed like our original agreement went out the window. When I told him "no" he started screaming that he was unappreciated and that we had just "used" him, accusing us of only caring about the money and not the client. After he stormed out, I had no idea what to do. I had never thought to ask Rob to get a non-compete clause, so he went directly to the MI company and told them that he had designed the entire program! And they believed him!

5. Do you feel manipulated, controlled, or even lied to sometimes? Does this person attempt to get what she wants by making you responsible for her feelings (e.g., "If you don't let me go to the rock concert I swear I'll hate you for the rest

of my life." Or, "Only an ungrateful and selfish daughter would rather stay at school for Christmas instead of coming home.")

Sarah's response: *To outsiders, my mother appears to be a highly educated college professor. But my life was a never-ending nightmare of her manipulation, control, and abuse. Some things I remember:*

* *I was never allowed to express anger to my mother, question or disobey her, and was punished severely whenever I broke these rules.*

* *At age fifteen, I awoke to go to school only to discover that my makeup and contact lenses were missing. My mother refused to return them to me until I "apologized" for something I had said the night before.*

* *At seventeen, I refused to do some household chores because I had to study for an exam the following day (I was a straight A, honor student). My mother flew into a rage and slapped me.*

* *My mother falsely informed the students in the college course she was teaching that my boyfriend had raped me and given me a venereal disease—I learned this later from one of the students in that class.*

* *When I refused to run an errand for her, she dumped an extremely expensive bottle of my perfume in the toilet.*

* *When I told her I had discussed marriage with my now-husband, and that he didn't feel ready, she called him at work and told him I was suicidal because he didn't want to marry me.*

* *When my father gave her just three presents at Christmas a few years ago (they had agreed to spend less money), she cornered me and went into a hysterical sobbing fit about how cruel he was. She stated that she wasn't going to say anything, though, because she didn't want to ruin anyone's Christmas (except mine, I guess).*

6. Does this person seem to demand constant attention? Is everything always about her—say, even your personal medical decisions? For example, can your borderline sister politely attend a birthday party when the focus is on someone else? Or will she push through people's boundaries and create a scene that will bring the attention back to her?

   Andy's response: *Sometimes I can't believe how self-centered my wife is. When I had to get a biopsy, she complained because we had to cancel a Halloween party. Then, when my father died and I had to leave suddenly for his funeral, she complained that I was leaving "so suddenly" and she would be alone. If I mentioned this to anyone, I don't know if they'd believe me.*

7. Are you afraid to ask for things in the relationship because this person will tell you you're selfish and demanding? Does this person imply, explicitly declare, or show by example that your needs are not as important as his?

   Marcia's response: *Since our son got married to a woman (Nell) whom I suspect has BPD, she has done all she can to alienate us from him. Once Nell and my husband had an argument about something—I think it was a last-minute babysitting job. Although we wanted very much to see our grandson, we just couldn't take care of him because we had plans. My husband finally got fed up with feeling manipulated and said no, and Nell screamed at him and slammed down the phone. We feel like we've lost our son and grandchild, and the pain is unbearable. We don't know what to do. My son just seems mesmerized by her and isn't willing to take a stand.*

8. Does this person continually contradict your needs and opinions so he can be the voice of authority? Do you feel that his expectations of you are constantly changing, so you can never do anything right?

   Linda's response: *I am always in a no-win situation with my borderline husband. If I take the kids to lessons and soccer, I am ignoring him and pressuring the kids. If I don't, I'm accused of not "offering them enough experiences." If I call him at his home office, I am intruding. If I don't, he says I must not love him. If I get him a present he always exchanges it. If I don't, I'm self-absorbed and "don't care." We make decisions and he gets mad when I do what we said I would do. I can't take much more of this.*

9. Are you accused of doing things you never did and saying things you never said? Do you feel misunderstood, and when you try to explain, do you find that the other person doesn't believe you?

   Kwan's response: *My sister was coming to San Francisco to visit me. We were talking about me taking off work when I reminded her that I was working "summer hours" and already had Friday afternoon off. Suddenly she started screaming uncontrollably and hung up on me. I tried to call back and she did the same thing. Finally I found out she was interpreting my statement about summer hours to mean "that's all I'm going to take off." I didn't say that, and didn't mean that, but she refused to let me explain.*

10. Do other people remark that the BP is verbally and emotionally abusive or encourage you to leave the relationship? But if you do try to leave, does the other person attempt to prevent you from leaving by trying to convince you no one else loves you more or could put up with someone like you?

    Harry's response: *My girlfriend goes though a pattern you can set a clock by. First comes the "I love you" part where everything is wonderful. That's what keeps me in the relationship. Then comes the "you're crowding me" speech, and the tension builds until she says she wants to break up. We do. Then three days later she calls as though* *nothing had happened. I have never seen this kind of behavior before. When things are good, they're great. But why does this cycle keep happening?*

11. Do you have a hard time planning social engagements, vacations, and other activities because the other person's moodiness, impulsiveness, or unpredictability may destroy your plans at the last minute? Do you make excuses for her behavior in an attempt to convince others (and yourself) that this is okay?

    Holly's response: *It's been a tradition in our family that Thanksgiving is celebrated at our house. But each year I dread it more. Our daughter Kaye, who's been a parenting challenge since birth, recently turned twelve. For the last couple of years, she's managed to ruin what used to be my favorite holiday. As the meal approaches and the number of cousins, siblings, and in-laws coming over increases, so does her manic behavior—she laughs wildly even though no one's made a joke, she shouts obscenities across the table, and makes lewd sexual advances to every male within reach. If someone else becomes the center of attention, she either sulks or goes into a fury so that, once again, she's in the spotlight.*

This Action Step was not a scientific study. But it had several goals:

* By looking at your answers and examining your feelings as you recalled examples from your own life, you should have a better idea if the person in your life has BPD traits and how they affect you.

* Some non-BPs have a hard time getting in touch with their angry or negative feelings. This Action Step hopefully helped you connect with your hidden emotions by putting you in touch with how other people have been affected.

* Speaking of emotions, what is most important in this workbook is how the BP's actions make you feel, not the presence or absence of a diagnosis. Only a qualified clinician can make a diagnosis. But anyone can use the steps in this book to improve their relationship, no matter what the diagnosis.

Help Is Available Now

One of the most healing things you can do is to join an online support group with people who have been through your situation and have come out of the other side of the tunnel. It may take you weeks, months, or years to apply the information in this workbook to your own life. (In fact, some people use the chaos the BP creates to distract them from their own problems.) But remember, *you're not alone on this journey.* You have this workbook, the original *Stop Walking on Eggshells,* and other helpful books, and, if you choose, an entire cyberspace community of more than a thousand people who understand exactly what you're going through. (A list of

Internet support groups is located at www.BPDCentral.com and in appendix A.) If you join, the members will share their experiences, help you sort out your many choices, and validate you; that is, acknowledge, believe, and value you and your point of view. Now that we know what BPD looks like from your point of view, let's see what the clinicians have to tell us.

Chapter 2

Defining BPD: The *DSM-IV* and Cognitive Distortions

When people ask me what BPD is, I just tell them that a high-functioning BP can be like Joan Crawford in Mommie Dearest *on the outside with the vulnerability of Marilyn Monroe on the inside.*

—R.K.

*J*anice Cauwels' book *Imbroglio* (1992) takes 172 pages to define Borderline Personality Disorder. And those 172 pages didn't come easily. Cauwels says that although she was referred to BPD researchers and clinicians by their peers, some refused to be interviewed because they didn't believe that a layperson could effectively and accurately write about such a complex disorder. Although some clinicians were pleased that someone was taking an interest in the disorder, others refused to speak to her or take her calls.

The Benefits of Understanding BPD

Let's discuss why understanding this disorder is important. In general, the better you understand BPD, the more you will understand how it has affected you in the past, how it could affect you in the future, and how you can help the BP and the rest of your family. With enough information and the ability to look at the world from the BP's point of view, you can even predict how certain situations may bring out the best (or the worst) from the BP in your life. Understanding BPD can be difficult. But it's worth it.

BPD in the New Millennium

Today, mental health professionals are more willing to discuss BPD with health writers. But Borderline Personality Disorder is so complex and has so many faces that mental health professionals still don't thoroughly understand what it is, what causes it, or how to treat it. This chapter will go over the *DSM-IV* (APA 1994) definition which is by far the most popular but leaves out many important traits. I will then examine some important BPD beliefs or cognitive distortions. This will help to give you a fuller picture of BP.

What Is a Personality Disorder?

Borderline Personality Disorder is just one of several personality disorders listed in the *DSM-IV*. While "desirable" and "normal" personality traits vary from culture to culture and change over time, a strong personality can be termed a "personality disorder" when it meets these criteria: "An enduring pattern of inner experience and behavior that deviates markedly from the expectations of the individual's culture" (1994, 629). Please note that cultures vary a great deal. Even in the same country, what is acceptable and what is not changes from generation to generation and is still defined in part by age, gender, social status, and ethnicity. But all personality disorders must meet the following standards:

* *The traits must be **longstanding** (i.e., several years).*

* *The behaviors must be **intense** (i.e., beyond the realm of "ordinary"). In other words, a reasonable person might be disappointed, angry, or sad if their*

partner decided to spend some of his vacation days bonding with his fishing buddies instead of planning a romantic getaway. Someone with BPD, however, might bar the door and explicitly or indirectly threaten to harm themselves or the partner if he leaves.

* *The behaviors must be **pervasive*** (i.e., running through most relationships, or at least with close family members). So a person who displays BPD traits only in front of his mother-in-law would not meet the clinical definition for BPD.

Personality disorder traits are deeply ingrained in the people who have them. Treatment is usually based on medication that helps with moodiness and depression, as well as psychotherapy that helps the client understand how old patterns are damaging and works with the client to develop healthier, more effective coping methods.

The *DSM-IV* Definition of BPD

To diagnose a person with BPD, practitioners follow the *DSM-IV* (APA 1994) definition:

Borderline Personality Disorder is a pervasive pattern of instability of interpersonal relationships, self-image, and affects [moods], and marked impulsivity beginning by early adulthood and present in a variety of contexts, as indicated by five (or more) of the following:

1. Frantic efforts to avoid real or imagined abandonment. Note: Do not include suicidal or self-mutilating behavior covered in (5).

2. A pattern of unstable and intense interpersonal relationships characterized by alternating between extremes of idealization and devaluation.

3. Identity disturbance: markedly and persistently unstable self-image or sense of self.

4. Impulsivity in at least two areas that are potentially self-damaging (e.g., spending, sex, substance abuse, shoplifting, reckless driving, binge eating). Note: Do not include suicidal or self-mutilating behavior covered in (5).

5. Recurrent suicidal behavior, gestures, or threats, or self-mutilating behavior.

6. Affective instability due to a marked reactivity of mood (e.g., intense episodic dysphoria, irritability, or anxiety usually lasting a few hours and only rarely more than a few days). [Dysphoria is the opposite of euphoria. It's a mixture of depression, anxiety, rage, and despair.]

7. Chronic feelings of emptiness.

8. Inappropriate, intense anger or difficulty controlling anger (e.g., frequent displays of temper, constant anger, recurrent physical fights).

9. Transient, stress-related paranoid ideation or severe dissociative symptoms.

Note that to be diagnosed with BPD, a person needs to display at least five of the nine traits in the *DSM-IV* list. If the BP in your life is under age eighteen, the child can be diagnosed if the BPD traits have persisted for at least one year and the behavior cannot be better accounted for by a normal developmental stage, the effects of substance abuse, or a more transient condition, such as depression or an eating disorder (1994).

📖 *Action Step 4:*
Does Your Loved One Fit the BPD **DSM-IV** *Criteria?*

Review the *DSM-IV* definition, and think about the person in your life who may display some or all of these traits. Which traits characterize him? Write them down in your notebook.

Even if your loved one displays five or more traits listed in the *DSM-IV*, remember only a qualified, competent clinician can make an accurate diagnosis or should tell someone they may have BPD. But if you answered "yes" to the questions opening this workbook and recognize your loved one in five or more these BPD traits, the information in this workbook should be helpful to you.

I realize that if you're reading this book, it's probably because the BP in your life won't admit to having a problem. The following stories from BPs who are willing to talk may help give you some insight into how it feels from the inside. Again, as with all the examples in this workbook, the stories and characters are actually composites of real people and situations. Some of the stories may illustrate more than one trait. For example, "Melissa's" story below shows both fear of abandonment and impulsivity.

Examples of BP Traits

1. Frantic efforts to avoid real or imagined abandonment.

> **Melissa, a BP:** *The past two years have been hell for me. It really became evident when my husband left me without warning (I almost don't blame him), although I should have left him years before. I remained in a physically and verbally abusive relationship because I was afraid of being alone. I immediately became involved with another man, but it was more of a sexual addiction. I found myself doing perverse things just to have a shred of "intimacy" back in my life. I begged the second man not to leave me. Since our breakup, I have done some terrible things to get revenge, even broken the law. I had over seventy sex partners by the time I was nineteen.*

2. A pattern of unstable and intense interpersonal relationships characterized by alternating between extremes of idealization and devaluation. This is called "splitting."

Mia, a non-BP: *A year ago, I volunteered to help out at a local nature center. Because my background is in forestry, I became a leader by default. When the kids came on a field trip from different parts of the city, they would call me to take the group on the trails. Well, another volunteer became extremely jealous. So she started to make subtle sarcastic remarks designed to put me down. Then she would take real incidents involving me, put a negative spin on them, and blow them up until they were unrecognizable. Finally I found out she was telling people that I was having an affair with one of the employees. Despite my protestations that this was untrue, the nature center kicked me out. And guess who they picked to replace me? Her. It was months before I realized this other woman had carefully orchestrated a distortion campaign against me. I couldn't take it anymore and left. About six months later, things blew up when she accused one of the volunteers of "stalking" her. This time people didn't just take her word for it—probably because she tried to ruin the reputation of someone who everyone knew and respected. Plus, she was dumb enough to accuse the man of stalking her at a time when he wasn't even in town. So she was asked to leave. I don't know if they finally recognized what she did to me. It's too late anyway.*

3. Markedly and persistently unstable self-image or sense of self.

Rachel, a BP: *For years, I'd handled my lack of identity managed with a rotating series of facades— never quite certain of who I was—but my passionate intensity had somehow numbed the uncertainty, distracting me and enabling me to get by. In the most difficult times, there had always been a bottle of tequila, a freshly rolled joint, a one-night stand, to dull the edges of confusion and self-disgust. I had handled the perennial question of who I was by avoiding it, by running, by never sitting still long enough to let it take root and drive me into despair. In essence, I had found a solution to the angst of my identity crisis by slowly destroying whomever and whatever I was. (Reiland 2002)*

4. Impulsivity in at least two areas that are potentially self-damaging.

Rachel, a BP: *Back then, I'd thought all of it was cool, my parents had been cool. Raising hell at school, getting loaded, getting high, screwing around—anything was fair play, as long as I was a "Stepford Child" at home.*

"They didn't give a shit, you know that?" I cried hysterically to my psychiatrist, Dr. Padgett. "I was crying for help, screaming for help, and they never did a thing! As long as my grades were top-notch, as long as I brought home the trophies and ribbons and plaques, brought home the glory—they didn't give a shit what else happened!"

Later, at home after the session, I went into the attic and retrieved a box with my mother's handwriting scrawled across it: "Rachel—Awards." That's all I was good for to them, I thought bitterly. Awards. I grabbed armloads of them, ribbons and parchment papers, and one by one, I crumpled them and threw them in the fireplace and lit a match. A bittersweet sensation of remorse and revenge filled me as I watched them blacken and turn to ash in the roaring flames. The words licked away, melted into oblivion, as the fire consumed them. Ribbon after ribbon after ribbon. Certificate after certificate. My high school diploma. All burned. Suddenly my husband walked in.

"What in the hell are you doing, Rachel!" he asked, shocked. (Reiland 2002)

5. Recurrent suicidal behavior, gestures, or threats, or self-harming behavior.

Amy, a BP: *I don't really want to die although I think about it all the time. I am just in so much emotional pain that suicide is the only thing I can think of to make it go away. I fantasize about how I would do it. I would want to have someone with me on the phone but not in the room so they could stop me. I mostly feel this way when I realize I am stuck in this borderline body and I can't change it. I can change my actions—some people think of me as very outgoing—but if someone says the wrong thing, my mood goes totally black. I feel trapped, and death is the only way out. I never self-harmed until one day I tried to see if it could take away the bad feelings without feeling suicidal. I took a punch pin and pricked it into my arm, all the while thinking what a horrible messed up person I must be. I hate hurting the people I love, some of whom will never trust me again because I've attempted suicide twice. I never knew how hurt and angry they would be. So now when I feel bad, I drink until I knock myself out. I know it's not good, but it's better than dying.*

6. Intense moodiness, irritability, anxiety, rage, and despair.

Kelly, a BP: *I lost my mother several years ago in a car accident. I haven't really gotten over that. Then my girlfriend broke up with me last Easter, about three months ago. I tried therapy and an antidepressant, and that worked for a while. Some days I want to kill myself and other days I want to kill someone else. I am pretty harmless aside from an occasional outrage—I would never really hurt anyone. I get really frustrated when something is out of my control. I react badly and am embarrassed that I get so mad. I wish I weren't so sensitive. I want everyone to know that borderline feelings are not much more than bizarre exaggerations of normal feelings and behavior.*

7. Chronic feelings of emptiness.

Rachel, a BP: *I fear the hole in the earth of nothingness, where once something else had stood. Even if I were able to "let go" with my psychiatrist and tear down the framework of my borderline feelings and perceptions, what would take its place? If I can't rely on the familiar, what can I rely upon? How would I handle the state of limbo, of nothingness? What else might I lose forever? My sense of humor? My assertiveness? My fighter attitude that kept me alive thus far? What would I be like if the borderline rage that had fueled me for so long were torn down and taken away? (Reiland 2002)*

Jason, a BP (age seventeen): *I don't fit in anywhere. I don't have any real friends and no one gives a shit about me or anything I do. All my parents care about is whether or not I'm on drugs (I'm not). The kids at school are applying for colleges or else they're all worked up about is who is dating who and whether we'll win the state* *championship. I really don't care what happens. It's all so pointless—besides, I probably won't even be alive for graduation. Whatever.*

8. Inappropriate, intense anger or difficulty controlling anger.

> **Byron, a BP:** *I think that borderlines feel rage when they're afraid . . . afraid of losing control, afraid the other person will leave them, and a sense that life just hasn't been fair. Or it's because we're hurting so intensely and no one knows how we hurt that we just externalize the pain we're feeling. Sometimes I'm really angry at someone, but I can't yell at them, so I yell at someone else. I have a code word with my family. When they use it, it means, "I love you, I hear you, I validate you, but I will talk to you when you are able to converse, not yell at me." When a BP is raging, he cannot hear you.*

9. Stress-related paranoid or severe dissociative symptoms that come and go. (Dissociation is a feeling of unreality, or "spacing out," that characterizes BPD.)

> **Sherry, a BP:** *I've used dissociation to cope with life for a long time—way before I understood the meaning of the word. When I was in grade school and kids were picking on me, I just blanked out. I blanked out during math, when my parents were arguing, or when my mother was yelling at me—which she did a lot. She called me names and criticized me for not living up to her expectations (which I now know was to meet her emotional needs, not vice versa). There are periods of my life I just don't remember. I got Ds in high school even though my IQ is 130. Sometimes a smell or color will bring up painful memories. Now that I know I do this, I wish I could just turn it off. I lose keys, people call me "spacey," and I forget errands—I have to write everything down. It causes problems in my relationships.*

The *DSM-IV* model you've just reviewed shows how BPD is defined by the American Psychiatric Association. While it is useful, in my experience it is flawed.

*   It omits some essential traits of borderlines such as feelings of shame, difficulty being alone, difficulty remembering the love people have for them when they're not around (called "poor object relations"), poor boundaries (both maintaining their own and respecting others'), control issues, the ability to be very competent in some situations and not in others, narcissistic demands (self-centeredness), and the lack of sophisticated methods to get what they want or need (which people often perceive as manipulation).

*   The magic number "five" is not scientifically based. Furthermore, it is imprecise, since five out of nine traits can be mathematically assembled in thousands of way and the same traits can be expressed differently from person to person (Sanderson and Widiger 1995).

*   It doesn't really explain the complex interactions between BPs and others in their lives. I will cover this in the next two chapters.

📖 *Action Step 5: Criteria for Children*

If your BP is a child, you may want to have some psychological testing done. The Gunderson Diagnostic Interview for Borderlines (DIB), which must be administered by a qualified professional, measures a child's social adaptation, impulsivity, emotions, connection to reality, interpersonal skills, and relationships. Anecdotally, several hundred parents in an Internet support group have differentiated normal child development from BPD behavior. The list of criteria below for BPD children reflects their insight. Rate your child from 1 (very characteristic) to 5 (very uncharacteristic) using the following criteria, if your child:

_____ Appeared "not normal" from a very early age

_____ Holds grudges and slights longer than most kids

_____ Is less affected by typical parental punishment

_____ Is adept at embellishing stories and even lying

_____ May have had some early form of childhood trauma (even before he could talk), especially involving separation from a parent

_____ Is super-sensitive to stimulation (noise, scratchy clothing)

_____ Is a poor sleeper

_____ Has poor concentration

_____ Seems to have no conscience

_____ Needs extra attention

Distorted Beliefs and Emotions of BPs

In our Internet group Welcome to Oz, we use the Oz metaphor (that strange place where monkeys fly, the people are tiny, and witches can be beautiful) to help us remember that, in essence, BPs live in a different world. Reminding ourselves of this helps us remember that we need to learn the culture, language, religion, and social norms of Oz. Before you criticize someone you need to walk a mile in their ruby red slippers.

📖 *Action Step 6:*
Does the BP in Your Life Hold These Beliefs?

Reading through the following traits and examples, think about whether or not the BP in your life has said or done something that shows she holds these beliefs. Look for actions that suggest self-destruction, feelings of being left out, low self-esteem, and a difference between what she says and what she does. In the space provided, write down an appropriate number, from 1 to 5, to rate the strength of the belief. A "1" indicates a strong belief in the distortion, a "3" either neutral or unknown, and a "5" is a strong disbelief in the distortion. Explain any 1s or 2s in your notebook. Again, the stories below are composite portraits of real people.

BPD Beliefs

_____ 1. "I am worthless, empty, and unlovable."

These BPD beliefs make BPs sensitive to remarks that could be construed as criticism (ironic, isn't it?)—which they deal with by either projecting the vitriol onto you or internalizing it, perhaps by doing something self-destructive.

High-functioning BPs can put on a mask of sorts that says, "I'm doing just fine here!" But no matter what either of you do, the feelings of worthlessness and shame eventually must be expressed again.

> **Brendan, a BP:** *I've always felt different. I remember in kindergarten being scared of the other kids in the class—afraid of what they could do or say to me. So I said nothing, which people interpreted to mean I was stuck up. We moved a lot of times when I was a kid and the same thing happened every time. I was the class "nerd" whom no one liked or would even speak to. When I look at pictures of myself I realize I wasn't a bad-looking kid. But I felt like a piece of scum, and in many ways I still do. I don't know if you can erase twelve years of being humiliated, kicked, called names, and ignored.*

_____ 2. "I am a terrible person and need to be punished."

This belief can be obvious or deduced from watching how the BP treats herself and others. Some BPs make up for their lack of self-love by overcompensating, fooling people into thinking they are overly self-confident, happy, powerful, and professional. Others project their feelings of worthlessness onto others. And some let other people abuse them because they feel they deserve it.

> **Mary, who has a BP sister:** *I don't understand why my sister doesn't stand up for herself more often. She tells me her husband won't "let her" work or give her enough money. She is a perfectly capable accounting manager. Why does she let this guy run her life and ruin every family gathering with his crass behavior? She's the original doormat.*

_____ 3. "If people love me, there must be something wrong with them."

This belief is almost never stated explicitly. Instead, the BP may go from one relationship to another, supposedly to find the "right" person. But the problem may be that the BP is afraid of getting too close and letting people really know him. This also can happen with therapists. If a therapist is good at recognizing the BP's true issues, the BP may suddenly find fault with the therapist and switch to someone else who is more agreeable with his views.

Grant, who has a BP girlfriend: *My girlfriend thinks she's fat and ugly and frequently asks me how she looks. I tell her she's beautiful because she is, inside and out. But she focuses on every flaw and holds it up to God's microscope and is never satisfied. Then she met a guy who said she could stand to lose a few pounds. Next thing I know she is sleeping with him. I can't believe she would do this to herself and us.*

_____ 4. "Feelings create facts, not the other way around."

To a great extent, we all make decisions based on emotions and then use our logic to rationalize them. But BPS can serve as judge and jury and come up with decisions that have no basis in reality. While most of us may be aware of how emotions affect our thoughts, the BP may not be able to separate the two. Thus, some decisions are impulsive instead of built on a solid foundation.

Harriet, who has a BP friend: *My friend Amy often says that I do a good job raising my kids—better than her. I don't think you can make comparisons, but she does. One day, my oldest son became captain of the soccer team, and Amy flew into a rage. She decided without a shred of evidence that the coach liked my son more than hers, and that's why my son was named captain. It was obviously jealousy. But what scares me is that she really believes it, and now she's publicly suggesting that I had a hand in this. When I ask her why, she just tells me she "knows."*

_____ 5. "Everything is black or white. No shades or other colors exist."

Splitting is one of the hallmarks of borderline traits: the inability to see middle ground on almost any subject, from a political issue to themselves to the behavior of the host at a party. Splits may last a long time—years—or they may last for only three minutes. All-or-nothing thinking pervades almost every area of a BP's life and complicates other BPD issues. The cliché about borderlines is that they put people up on pedestals merely to knock them down.

Patricia, who has a BP daughter and a mother: *We adopted our granddaughter Deborah because her mother (our daughter) was too emotionally unstable to care for her. Now we're worried because at eleven, Deborah seems unable to see people in tones of gray. She bolts from friendship to friendship, and the pattern is always the same: At first the new friend is more than perfect, a soul mate, the best thing that ever happened. But then suddenly something goes wrong. Deborah can't find a nice thing to say about the girl and goes out of her way to trash her as hurtfully as possible. She treats us the same way: Either we're wonderful and she can't hug us enough, or we're evil incarnate and she looks at us with pure hate.*

_____ 6. "I am the victim of everyone else's behavior."

The black-and-white thinking that goes with splitting also means that BPs split themselves into "all good" or "all bad." To avoid feeling all bad, BPs often deny their own involvement in life's unhappy consequences. Every disappointment is someone else's fault. For example, it's common on the Internet for people to act inappropriately, then harass e-mail list facilitators who suspend or moderate them for breaking the guidelines. One woman I know not only broke the guidelines but forcibly tried to take control of a list by deceiving the list software provider. It didn't work. But three years later, she still paints herself as the poor, hapless victim and conducts distortion campaigns (plants false negative information) about the facilitators—even though she was the one who actually chose to leave. To most BPS, feelings equal facts, not the other way around. Non-BPs whose borderline partners decide to leave the relationship often find that their former partners blame *them* for "abandoning them."

> **Sylvie, a BP:** *I can't believe that I took all that time out of my schedule to give my feedback on this new waste-to-energy project in Seattle. I had to get up at 6 A.M. and wait for two hours at the airport, where it's always a madhouse. Technically, I was there and being paid for my expenses, which is what I agreed to. The only reason I even did it is because there was always the possibility of landing a job instead of just a consulting contract. I need the money. But when I got there, the president of the board had given the executive director job to someone else—an unqualified bitch who thinks she's something but is just an egotist with a crate of emotional problems. You can be sure I demanded all my expenses that very day, down to the Zinfandel I had on the plane. I would have made such a better executive director, but they'll never know it because once I learned I had come all that way for nothing, I stormed out of there. I hope the organization goes down the tubes, which it probably will without me there.*

_____ 7. "If I can control someone, they will love me."

BPs may feel so out of control of their emotional life that they try to exert complete control over their environment and the behavior of others, if they can. People who acquiesce to their demands are "loved" while those who don't are split into all bad.

> **Tamara:** *When I went to visit my mother after a major operation, she insisted that I eat dinner seated at the table even though I was in terrible pain. Then she complained about the way I ate at every meal. If she was cold, I had to wear a jacket. Everything had to be done her way, on her schedule. I'm forty years old and she still treats me like a child.*

_____ 8. "I need other people to be happy. But my need so scares me, I have to push them away."

This is also called the abandonment/engulfment cycle. If you get too close to the BP, she will feel trapped. If you're too far away, she'll feel abandoned. So the relationship becomes a continuous push-pull that Jerold J. Kreisman terms, "I hate you—don't leave me" (1989).

> **Rachel, a BP:** *A warmth, what I imagined a daughter loved by her father might feel, spread through my body on the drive home from my psychiatrist's office. Dr. Padgett thought I was lovable and courageous. Dr. Padgett was there for me. Therapy became a bittersweet addiction—moments of catharsis, moments when my soul lying hidden and aching was sought out and gently stroked by Dr. Padgett's love, moments of my*

long hunger being whetted with the sweet taste of love and understanding.

Yet, now I was alone. Four days of filler, killing time, going through the motions. Therapy was all that mattered. No, that wasn't true—being in his presence, feeling his acceptance, these were my desperate needs and they were met in transient moments. But when the next session came, I was numb from needing him too much. I said nothing.

"What's on your mind?" he asked.

"Nothing," I said. Minutes passed again.

"You're burying your feelings, Rachel. They are there, but we can't work on them unless you open up."

My power fed on itself, growing larger, omnipotent. Come on, Padgett. Grovel. Beg for it. Get on your knees.

"You're right, Dr. Padgett," I said. "There are things on my mind. But I have no intention of sharing them with you. Know why? Because you are a manipulative bastard, that's why! A control freak. You want me to get down on my hands and knees and strip my soul completely naked so you can exploit it. You want to see me grovel for your attention. Well, I'm not doing it. I don't need you. I don't need anybody. I wouldn't call you if you were the last person alive and I had a loaded gun pointed down my throat!" (Reiland 2002)

_____ 9. "If anyone really knew me, they would hate me."

This refers to the "all good" mask some BPs wear to avoid exposing their real feelings of shame, fear, and self-loathing.

Laura, a BP: *A lot of people tell me I'm a great singer. I get the solos. Well, la de da. I've had people ask for my autograph after concerts. They tell me how moved they were by my performance. But they don't know the real me, the one who all the kids teased in school, the one my parents abandoned, the one who used to have anorexia and weighed seventy-six pounds. They tell me I'm great and I lie on the bed sobbing my eyes out because no one really cares. No one knows the real me.*

_____ 10. "My mask of self-confidence will fool everyone."

The "all good" mask fools some people some of the time. But the BP can't sustain it forever. Many partners find that their perfect mate becomes a different person once the marriage license is signed.

Christopher, whose mother is a BP: *When my mother poses us for a family picture, she makes everyone smile as if we had a normal family life. People have no idea what she is like behind closed doors. One time she was raging at me in a shopping mall and suddenly she saw a friend. She stopped and said "hello," cheery as ever. And when the friend was out of earshot, she started in on me, right where she left off.*

_____ 11. "If I can prove you're a miserable excuse for a human being, that means I'm not as bad as I think I am."

BPs need an infinite amount of attention, love, or romance to make up for the self-love they lack. But they think of love as a finite resource and often become jealous of other people in their loved one's life. So they may try to cut friends and family members out of the non-BP's life so there's more love "left over." Or, they may seek to put others down because it makes them feel better about themselves. This can result in a constant stream of blame and criticism, for example, against their in-laws. The borderline doesn't want to "compete" for her spouse's love, so she tries to undermine the relationship between her husband and his parents. In-laws who can do their best to ignore this seemingly cruel behavior and go out of their way to include the daughter-in-law may have a better chance of maintaining a relationship with their son and any grandchildren.

> **Rhonda, a non-BP:** *The BP in my life, a colleague at the university, sent a mass e-mail accusing me of writing a scientific paper that was "full of lies and distortions." She said in the e-mail that she hadn't actually read the study, but she "knew from the title that it would be bad." I guess a few people chided her about writing a review based on the title, so she sent me a letter apologizing. I didn't respond right away because I wanted her to think about what she had done and I wasn't sure how to respond. But I never got a chance to react— twenty-four hours later, she threw a fit and wrote me an e-mail attacking me very personally for not "forgiving her" and accusing me of being a very conniving, manipulative person. Then she went on the Internet and started posting trash about me in a professional online group. This is the second time she has done something like this to me; I hear she does this to others, too.*

The Limbic System: How Illogical Beliefs Thrive

As a writer, I was once called upon to write a newsletter for a manufacturer of heating, cooling, and ventilation systems. When I met my contact at his cubicle to conduct the interview, I noticed that he could adjust the temperature, lighting, and even ambient noise right inside his space. When I commented on it, he said that his own company had invented it, but it was never marketed because a key person had come into power who didn't like the system's inventor. In other words, the president of the company refused to market a successful product because of his personal feelings for his predecessor.

We are all under the illusion that we are logical beings. But it's a myth. All of our opinions go through an emotional "filter" before they spring forth, seemingly born from logical reasoning. But the opposite occurs: we form an opinion emotionally (sometimes subconsciously) then rationalize it through logic. This is especially true for people with BPD. Some clinicians believe that the limbic systems of BPs do not work properly.

Jury consultant Jo-Ellan Dimitrius Ph.D., and Mark Mazzarella use extensive research to help their clients make a good impression on juries. In their book *Put Your Best Foot Forward: Make a Great Impression by Taking Control of How Others See You* (2000), they explain how our limbic system (the emotional center of the brain) helps us make unconscious decisions about other people. Simplified, the limbic system is composed of three main parts—the thalamus, hypothalamus, and amygdala—that regulate the "fight or flight" instinct and sex drive, store memory and provide meaning to that memory, and help us suppress emotional or instinctive impulses. "When we lose rational control, the amygdala has been overwhelmed. Even with extensive psychotherapy it is often impossible to determine why events may trigger emotional reactions that are so powerful our normal control systems fail. The explanation often lies beyond our capacity to know, because events may have occurred in our early childhood and been recorded emotionally . . . long before our rational brain developed sufficiently to recognize them" (25–26).

The Implications of this Knowledge

"Every person you meet has his own [emotional response] and will remember those aspects of your personality or behavior that make an emotional impact. They will be noticed first, considered the most important, and be remembered the longest" (Dimitrius and Mazzarella 2000, 29). Thus, your attraction to people who have BPD may be based on things that happened before you met. It may be the reason so many people who had BPD mothers marry borderlines: it feels familiar and "right," and subconsciously we may hope to come to closure with unfinished business from our past. Knowing what triggers various emotions in you and in the BP in your life can help you better manage interactions. At least, you'll be able to anticipate possible problems earlier.

In this chapter, we looked at the *DSM-IV* definition of BPD and reviewed some cognitive distortions, or illogical ways BPs look at the world. I also pointed out that everyone—not just BPs—"thinks" more with their emotions than their intellect. Since BPs can act very differently, in the next chapter I'll describe a way of sub-categorizing BPD behavior.

Chapter 3

Defining BPD: The Subtypes

I just came across BPDCentral this morning. I had no idea other people had a mother like mine. I feel like Tarzan the first time he saw another human being.

—a woman on the Internet

*B*PD would be much more recognized and understood by both clinicians and the public if everyone with the disorder acted the same way. But one of the chief difficulties of understanding BPD is that two people with the disorder can act in opposite ways.

BPs are the same as everyone else—different stimuli can make people act in totally different ways. Think for a moment about the people who have a loved one who has been killed by a drunk driver. Some family members demand vengeance; others forgive. Some family members never quite get on with their lives; others found non-profit organizations to combat the problem of drunk driving. And, of course, these are just a couple of examples of how people react in this situation. In real life, the variables are endless. But the stimulus—the preventable loss of a loved one—is the same.

Researchers don't know why BP behavior is so diverse, but theorize that it depends upon a variety of factors, such as brain chemistry, the supportive people in the BP's life, the degree of external or internal pressure, triggering situations, and early environmental factors.

Classifying BPD by Functioning and Behavior Types

Clinicians recognize the differences between the way BPs behave, but they don't all agree on the subtypes or why some BPs fall in one subgroup while others fall into another. In *Stop Walking on Eggshells*, Paul Mason, M.S., and I simplified the matter by categorizing people with BPD as being on a continuum from low-functioning, acting–in to high-functioning, acting-out (Mason and Kreger 1998). These two types can be so different it's almost as if they're two different disorders. Like our earlier example, these are just polar opposites; in real life, BPS are usually a blend of the two with one type predominating.

Higher-functioning, acting-out BPs. These BPs are able to work, do not self-harm or make suicide attempts, and otherwise maintain a façade of normalcy that crumbles around family members. With those close to her, the BP may project her low self-worth onto others through acting out, or raging, blaming, criticizing, and otherwise convincing family members to feel these painful feelings for her. She does not generally seek professional help because she believes that everyone else has a problem.

A high-functioning borderline child brings home straight As, makes the track team, and plays trumpet in the school band. All her teachers think she's perfect. Yet, she never has the same best friend for more than a month, the family pets are afraid of her, and she has multiple scars in places covered by her clothes.

This kind of behavior usually causes non-BPs to lose their self-esteem, feel dependent on the BP, worry about the effect of the BP's behavior on others, and consider stopping contact with the BP. An example of this type of BP is the Joan Crawford character in *Mommie Dearest*.

Lower-functioning, acting-in types. This type of BP may be on disability, unemployed, or underemployed. Unlike the high-functioning, acting-out BP, he deals with his painful feelings of shame by self-harming or making suicide attempts, self-criticism, abusing medication, and other acts that hurt the BP himself directly (and others indirectly). These types of BPs often feel "different" from other people, believe they have problems, and seek help from mental health professionals. An example of this type of BP is Marilyn Monroe, who is probably the most often-mentioned BP in the literature.

A low-functioning, acting-in BP child may spend much of her life in hospitals or residential treatment centers in an attempt to keep her from cutting herself or doing other forms of self-harm.

Those who display characteristics of both: These BPs fall somewhere in the middle or only slightly to one side of the two basic types. A good example is Rachel Reiland (2002). Another is the late Princess Diana, whose BPD is detailed in several books. While she battled eating disorders, self-harm, depression, and displayed other low-functioning behavior, she managed to put in public appearances, work for charity causes, and parent her two sons very well.

📖 Action Step 7:
Where Is Your BP on the Continuum?

In what ways could the BP in your life be the higher-functioning, acting-out type, and in which major ways is he or she a lower-functioning, acting-in type? Circle the examples below that apply to your situation, and then add some of your own examples. If you're unsure of where a characteristic belongs, ask yourself if the behavior makes you worried about the BP (acting-in) or worried about you (acting-out). For functioning, ask yourself if the BP acted like this for several weeks or months, could he make it on his own? A "no" probably means lower functioning; a "yes" probably means higher acting.

* **High-Functioning/Acting-Out**	* **Low-Functioning/Acting-In**
* Episodes of raging	* Episodes of self-harm
* Holds a job, especially one with responsibility	* Threats of suicide or actual attempts
* Is capable of maintaining friendships	* Inability to hold a job for any length of time, or working below his or her capabilities
* Few people outside of the family know of problems	* Has trouble with daily living responsibilities such as shopping
* Can act "normal" when necessary	* Engages in unnecessarily dangerous activities

* Pushes other away more than vice versa

* Describes emotional pain

* Has a façade of perfection in all things

* Seeks therapy

* Looks at others as extensions of themselves rather than separate people with their own needs

* One mistake leads to feelings of overall failure

* Blames and criticizes others

* _____

* _____

* _____

* _____

* _____

* _____

* _____

    In chapter 5, we'll discuss how the needs of non-BPs are different depending on many factors, including where the BP lies on the continuum of functioning and behavior style.

The Lawson Method of Describing BPD Behavior

Clinician Christine Ann Lawson, Ph.D., recently developed four distinct types of BPs in her book *Understanding the Borderline Mother: Helping Her Children Transcend the Intense, Unpredictable, and Volatile Relationship* (2000).

    Lawson's book categorizes mothers into four groups: Witches, Queens, Hermits, and Waifs. "Queens" and "Witches" are higher-functioning, acting-out BPs, while "Hermits" and "Waifs" are lower-functioning, acting-in types. Most BPs display elements of all four categories.

    Although her book is about mothers, in a telephone conversation with me Lawson said her descriptions are applicable to both genders and all relationships, not just the parent-child relationship. Behavior toward children, of course, is more serious because children are unable to protect themselves and don't have an adult point of reference. Lawson types individuals based on their typical thoughts, emotions, and actions. In the following Action Step, I have taken this model and applied it to BPs in general.

📖 *Action Step 8: Queen, Witch, Waif, or Hermit?*

As you read the following descriptions, circle the traits, thoughts, emotions, and actions that seem to apply to the BP in your life. Use your notebook to write down your observations about the BP. You can also make notes at the end of the section to remind yourself why you circled that trait. Finally, count the circled items, reread the traits, and decide if any one of these descriptions apply to your loved one more than the others.

The Witch

Typical Thoughts

Unconsciously, Witches hate themselves because they grew up in an environment that "required complete submission to a hostile or sadistic caregiver" (Lawson 2000, 131). They continue the cycle by acting cruelly to others, especially those who are too weak, young, or powerless to help themselves.

Typical Emotions

They feel no remorse for nightmarish acts, showing more interest in their own well-being than concern over the way they've hurt others. The Witch's triggers include jealousy, criticism, betrayal, abandonment, feeling left out, and being ignored.

Typical Actions and Central Dilemma

Most BP parents do not physically abuse their children. Those who do probably fall into this category. However, the abuse usually occurs when other, competent adults are not present. Thus, family members can live in fear while all seems well to the outside world. Witches want power and control over others so that others do not abandon them. When someone or something triggers the Witch's abandonment fear, this BP can become brutal and full of rage, even punishing or hurting family members who stand in her way. These types of BPs are most resistant to treatment: they will not allow others to help and the source of self-loathing runs very deep.

Final number of circled items _____

The Queen

Typical Thoughts

"I want more attention. I *deserve* more attention. And, by the way, what have you done for me lately?" Also, "My children should fulfill my needs, not the other way around. They don't love or respect me if they disagree with me, go against my wishes, or have needs of their own."

Typical Feelings

These include entitlement, deprivation, emptiness, anger, frustration, or loneliness from the deprivation they felt as children. Queens are impatient and have a low tolerance for frustration. They also push others' boundaries without recognition or regret.

Typical Actions and Central Dilemma

Driven by feelings of emptiness and unable to soothe themselves, Queens do what it takes to get what they feel they so richly deserve. This includes vindictive acts like blackmail. Initially they may impress others with their social graces. But when "friends" can no longer deliver, the Queen cuts them off without a thought. Queens are capable of real manipulation (vs. more primitive BP defenses) to get what they desire.

The Waif

Typical Thoughts

"I am a worthless victim. I do so want to be loved and protected, but I am not worthy of it." Philosophy: The glass is not only half empty, but is about to spill all over the floor I just washed.

Typical Feelings

Helplessness, hopelessness, and despair. Rage can be masked by sadness and depression, but released by rejection or abandonment. Waifs distort their own errors or disappointments, leading to more shame. They feel vulnerable, defective, anxious, moody, and irrationally fearful.

Typical Actions and Central Dilemma

They look to others to "save them," but ultimately refuse assistance because helplessness makes them feel safe. Ironically, if they mistrust everyone and let no one get close, they stay in control and no one can abandon or disappoint them. Waifs may hurt themselves to express shame, but they are capable of raging if they feel rejected or abandoned. They don't ask for what they need, then appear martyr-like because others can't read their minds and give it to them. Waifs may have crying spells and be unable to nurture others.

Final number of circled items _____

The Hermit

Typical Thoughts

"It's a dog eat dog world out there and I'm a cat. Everyone out there is for themselves and no place is safe. Since people will always end up betraying me, I must be alert for hints or hidden meanings in things others would consider innocuous."

Typical Feelings

Terrified of not having control, fear of engulfment keeps them from obtaining comfort. No wonder they see potential disaster everywhere. Hermits take criticism as a global condemnation of themselves and depend upon work and hobbies for self-esteem. Their inner shame is expressed through their continual criticism of others.

Typical Actions and Central Dilemma

The hard shell makes these BPs appear confident, determined, independent, and even socially graceful. But it's a veneer. Like many BPs, hermits show one face to the world and another to everyone else. Close family members experience "distrust, perfectionism, insecurity, anxiety, rage and paranoia" (Lawson 2000, 80). They hold everyone to the same ideal of perfection, punishing others by raging or shutting them out. Hermits fear losing themselves, which translates into possessiveness about their belongings.

Final number of circled items _____

Which of these types, if any, reminds you most of the BP in your life? _____

_____

Which is the secondary type? _____

In upcoming chapters, I'll compare non-BP reactions to each type of Lawson's BPs: Queen, Witch, Hermit, and Waif.

How Does It Feel to Have BPD?

Up until now I've talked about what it's like to have BPD or be with someone who does. Now, I'd like you to try to imagine what it actually feels like to have BPD. Getting close to feeling your BP's emotions will help you predict his or her actions and reactions.

📖 Action Step 9:
The Courtroom Action Step

Imagine you have been accused of a serious crime. You have been arrested and tried, and now you're sitting in a courtroom waiting for the jury to return its verdict. They have been in conference for a few hours, and you're starting to get edgy and nervous. You're trying to figure out if a long deliberation is a good sign or a bad sign. Every time a door opens and someone walks into the courtroom, you jump. Then you see that it's only a court employee and you get irritated. You start feeling scared, but you try not to allow fear to surface because you think things will go better if you keep your confidence—but it's getting harder by the minute.

Without warning, you feel someone tugging on your sleeve from behind. You turn around to see who it is, and you find yourself looking into the face of an old friend who says, "I have an appointment this afternoon, and I need you to pick up my kids after school. Please don't tell me you're too busy."

Now, how do you feel?

Step 1. Put a check in the blank that describes how you think you might feel in such a situation:

_____ morose	_____ goaded
_____ unappreciated	_____ taken advantage of
_____ run over	_____ anxious
_____ tense	_____ vulnerable
_____ taken advantage of	_____ outraged
_____ alarmed	_____ scared
_____ angry	_____ frustrated
_____ humbled	_____ humiliated
_____ peaceful	_____ rested
_____ irate	_____ depressed
_____ sad	_____ on edge
_____ nervous	_____ hungry

Write your own feelings in the following blanks.

_____

_____

Step 2. Look over the list of emotions above, and think about what it would mean to have all of these feelings at once. Now use your imagination and think what it would be like if you had these feelings every day, off and on throughout the day. How would it affect your attitude toward people in authority? _____

_____

_____

How would it affect your attitude toward people who offer you any kind of comfort, sympathy, or kind understanding? _____

_____

_____

How do you think it would affect your attitude toward subordinates, someone over whom you have some power and/or authority? _____

_____

_____

Now, go back and put an "X" in the blank beside each word that is the opposite of what you might be feeling, e.g., I would be feeling anything *but* _____ (hungry, peaceful, etc.).

Some BPs castigate themselves, feeling shame and guilt for who they are or what they've done. In some cases the BP has actually done something to feel guilty for, but most feel ashamed of just existing (it's part of the definition of BPD). Because they see themselves as either all black or all white, any flaw can make them feel like a criminal awaiting the worst sentence possible: abandonment by those they love and count on. This Action Step is meant to help you feel what it's like to constantly feel under pressure, on edge, uneasy, and afraid. Behaviors that may confuse you are more understandable when you know the BP's frame of mind. For the BP, your everyday needs are the straw that broke the camel's back.

Feelings of Ambivalence

I've discussed some of the ways in which BPs feel ambivalent about the important people in their lives—for example, they need closeness and fear it at the same time. They may feel one way and act the opposite way to minimize their vulnerability. They want to be able to count on people and be given unconditional love, yet they detest the control it gives others over them. After all, in a moment the person the BP loves could walk away and leave them in a cold, annihilating black void. So at the same time they love, they seek to minimize or deny that need.

This is a problem we all face: balancing our need for others while maintaining our autonomy. But non-disordered people know that even if someone leaves us by choice or by death, we can grieve and still cope; still be alive. People with BPD feel that if others disappear, they will, too.

To use a metaphor, when we try to balance these issues, we do so through trial and error. Sometimes our hearts get broken, but we know we will eventually get over our loss. But people with BPD balance these issues on a tightrope fifty feet high with no safety net underneath: very little self-love, self-respect, hope, and memory of the good things about life to sustain them through the hard times.

This Action Step will help you understand that emotional state. The more imagination and real feeling you bring to it, the better.

📖 Action Step 10:
The Sinking Ship Action Step

First, come up with the name of a person you intensely dislike. Someone you absolutely detest, scorn, and despise—consider politicians you disagree with, a singer whose songs annoy you, a childhood bully, people who rob and rape, or even certain sports teams (or members thereof). If you can, imagine that this person dislikes you as much as you dislike him. (If you have such peace and love in your heart that you cannot find anyone on earth to despise, bless you—the planet needs more people like you.) Imagine that person at their most loathsome. Conjure up the way they speak, look, and even smell, if you can. Picture his smiling face (or sneer) in the newspaper, book jacket, or right in front of you.

Once you feel sufficiently full of revulsion, imagine that you are taking a lovely vacation cruise to the Bahamas. The cruise ship hits an iceberg and starts to sink. (Don't argue that there are no icebergs near the Bahamas—use your imagination!) You hastily grab a life jacket and swim away from the ship as it sinks beneath the surface of the water. You look around, but you can't see anything but fog. You're alone.

Time passes. You worry if sharks linger here, and you're thirsty. Fresh water is all you can think about. Night falls (the water is warmer in the Bahamas, of course) and you yell for help until you are hoarse. Apparently you have drifted away from all the lifeboats and other survivors. Nobody answers. You can hear seagulls calling, feel the waves lapping against your chin, and taste the salt in your mouth. Morning comes, and just as the sun comes up, you see a boat approaching. You wipe the salt crust off your mouth and hoarsely yell for help again, and—yes, thank God—the captain sees you. You have never felt so elated to see another human being in your life.

But as the boat approaches you, the sneering face of that person you despise comes into focus. He or she is not only *on* the boat—this person you loathe is *captain* of the boat and can choose to pick you up or leave you to die. You absolutely can't stand the fact that you are going to owe this person your life, but the thought of death is not a pleasant one either.

Now think carefully about how you would react to seeing your enemy about to rescue you and put a check mark next to the statement below that best characterizes your feelings. You can check off as many as you want. Don't worry if your answers conflict with each other.

1. I would keep on drifting and think, "I'd rather drown than be rescued by *that* person!"

    ____ Totally disagree

    ____ Disagree

    ____ Neither agree nor disagree

    ____ Agree

    ____ Totally agree

2. I would grit my teeth, shut my mouth, and climb on board the boat.

    ____ Totally disagree

    ____ Disagree

    ____ Neither agree nor disagree

    ____ Agree

    ____ Totally agree

3. I would grit my teeth, shut my mouth, climb on board the jerk's boat, and decide I'll tell this person what I really think once I'm safely back on dry land and get some water.

    ____ Totally disagree

    ____ Disagree

    ____ Neither agree nor disagree

    ____ Agree

    ____ Totally agree

4. I would just be grateful that I'm being rescued and forget about whose boat it is.

    ____ Totally disagree

    ____ Disagree

    ____ Neither agree nor disagree

    ____ Agree

    ____ Totally agree

    ____ Totally agree

Intellectually, you know you can't "totally agree" with more than one sentiment because you can't act two ways at the same time. But your emotions have no IQ: they can feel a dozen things at once. If you felt any sense of being torn between two diametrically opposed reactions, that is akin to what someone with BPD feels much of the time. The common term for that condition is *ambivalence*, and that term is used clinically to describe a person who is in that mental state very often, no matter what the circumstances are. Does it feel uncomfortable? Imagine what it would be like to live that way most of the time, and you can get an idea of what it feels like to have BPD. It's one reason why BPs act so inconsistently and change their opinions or wishes so often.

Reminding Yourself of the Good Qualities of the BP

Sometimes in discussing the difficult parts of caring about someone with BPD, we miss the main point: if we didn't love him and care about her future, we wouldn't be trying so hard to understand, communicate, and find a treatment for BPD.

It can be difficult to separate the person from the disorder. Thus this Action Step will remind you why the BP isn't the only person who feels ambivalent. It's tempting to look at the BP's personality and discount negative or hurtful traits. But both are part of the BP's complex personality.

📖 Action Step 11: *Accentuate the Positive*

Looking at the good qualities listed below, circle the ones that characterize the BP in your life. Circle the ones most important to you, and write in any that are missing. Then, in your notebook, write down two or three of the times you remember feeling close and connected with this person.

Artistic	Attractive	Compassionate
Competent	Creative	Cultured
Dedicated	Fun	Generous
Good sense of humor	Helpful	Intelligent
Interesting	Kind	Polite
Enthusiastic	Friendly	Shared history
Shared hobbies	Skilled	Spontaneous
Talented	Unafraid	Witty
Loving	Outgoing	Enthusiastic

Friendly   Outgoing   Polite

_____   _____   _____

As you read the rest of this workbook, try to see the whole person: the good points and the things you wish were different. Since the two sides of the person can be so far apart, it can be difficult to understand that the person you love has such negative as well as positive traits. But they are all part of the same person. And though it is difficult to integrate these two "selves," a BP who gets help from an experienced, qualified clinician can make the good times more frequent than the bad ones, and make the bad ones easier to handle.

Up until now, I've been looking at BPD like a primary color. Red is red is red. But when you mix red with other colors—i.e., friends and family members, each of whom have their own color—the interaction takes on a hue of its own. In the next chapter, we'll look at the dynamics of a relationship in which one or both of the parties has BPD.

Chapter 4

Getting Together: Relationship Behavior Patterns

My therapist told me that my wife gave Borderline Personality Disorder a bad name. When I asked her if she was crazy, the therapist said, "No, but she will make everyone around her crazy."

—from a member of the Welcome to Oz Internet support list

*J*ust like there are many ways of explaining BPD behavior, there are many ways of describing the dynamics between BP/non-BP partners, parents and their children, siblings, friends, and all other types of relationships. Each relationship is unique. But certain patterns and dynamics seem to repeat themselves within all BP and non-BP relationships.

📖 *Action Step 12:*
Identify BP/Non-BP Patterns in Your Life

The following patterns of behavior follow a predicable course much like thunder follows lightning. They stem from the nine borderline *DSM-IV* traits, as well as the false beliefs (cognitive distortions) outlined in chapter 2. While other books about BPD just analyze the "disordered" person, this workbook and *SWOE* (Mason and Kreger 1998) describe how the BP's emotions and behaviors affect you, how you respond, how that in turn affects the BP and the relationship, and how the cycle goes on.

The following exercises accomplish two objectives: they teach you the games borderlines play as well as your typical reaction to them. After the description of each "game," think carefully about how you would feel if you were the main character described in the example. Read the sample reactions that follow and choose the one that most closely describes what your reaction would be. You'll find discussions of each situation at the end of the chapter.

Tag, You're It: A Game of Projection

Projection is accusing other people of doing, saying, or believing something (often negative) that people do not want to acknowledge in themselves. The BP's unconscious hope is that by projecting this unpleasant stuff onto another person—by tagging someone else and making them "it"—he will feel better about himself. And the BP does feel better, for a little while. But the pain comes back. So the game is played again and again. The projection can be an exaggeration of something that has a basis in reality or it can be a total fabrication. Clinician James Paul Shirley says, "Projection is a core aspect of BPD. By recognizing the BP's projections, you can potentially gain a better understanding of their feelings, because whatever traits they project onto you will be the traits they see but cannot accept in themselves."

One list member said he finally understood projection when his wife threatened him physically during an argument. During their marriage counseling session a few days later, she told the therapist that *he* had made the threats—and his wife truly believed it.

George: *My wife Cyndi keeps telling me I am selfish because I want to look for a job in a new city. I've been looking here for eighteen months and I haven't found* *anything yet. But she wants to stay here where her parents live close by. I know that anything I find here won't be at the salary or management level I need. But if I even bring up the thought of moving, she tells me all I think about is my job, my job, my job, and I have no consideration for her and her feelings. She's a nurse and can find a job anywhere. But finding a job at my level in my field is almost impossible.*

Now, pretend you are George. Circle the letter next to the reaction that comes closest to how you would feel in this situation.

A. It's difficult to know what should be done but I would feel selfish and maybe even ashamed for badgering Cyndi to move. She loves her family and shouldn't have to move away from them. George should do what it takes to keep her happy. If I were him, I couldn't stand the disagreement and her being mad at me for very long.

B. I would be furious beyond belief if my wife called me selfish when it's obvious that *she's* being inflexible, childish, and totally self-centered. Cyndi is a grown-up and she won't even *consider* moving away from mommy and daddy. It's time to cut the apron strings.

C. I don't think George is being selfish. But he's not communicating well enough with his wife. Perhaps George can come up with a list of all the reasons why a move would make the most economic and personal sense for both of them and go through each point, one by one. If George's job pays enough, Cyndi can travel home frequently, and she'll have new friends in addition to her family.

D. Both George and Cyndi should think through their values and goals and come up with a solution that suits them both. They both may need to compromise.

Everything Is Your Fault

Continual blame and criticism is another defense mechanism that some people with BPD who act out use as a survival tool. The faultfinding may be pure fantasy on the BP's part or it can be an exaggeration of real-life problems. The BP of one man I interviewed raged at him for eating too quickly; another woman's husband so hated the way she ate that she refused to eat with the family and put up with his insults. Nothing is too small and petty for a BP who needs to put others down to feel better about himself.

In addition, BPs can sometimes tell or ask someone to do something, then blame them for doing what they asked. (This is also an example of a no-win situation.) The child of a BP was forced to share all of her toys with her friends, who would break them. Then the mother would blame the daughter for breaking her toys.

Joan: *I can't do anything right, according to my girlfriend Kathy. She complains about the way I dress, talk, eat, make the bed, my family, the way my family celebrates Christmas—anything that strays from the Kathy Bible of the Way Things Should Be. I don't like this about her, but I can't imagine leaving her. We do have lots of good times together and I love her.*

A. Joan should try to respect Kathy's feelings and accept her criticisms as expressions of love. If they have good times together, why throw away the whole relationship?

B. I can't imagine being with such a bitch. I would grab my stuff and get out of that relationship pronto.

C. If I were Joan I would try to reason with Kathy and gently show her that she's being illogical. I might explain that there is no "right" or "wrong about a lot of these things, just opinions and traditions. I'm sure Kathy will understand.

D. No one can stay very long in a relationship where one person runs over another one and keep their self-esteem. I would try to get Kathy into couples therapy to see why she believes that nothing Joan does is right. I would also examine what keeps me in this relationship.

My Needs Are Most Important

This is the narcissistic need of BPs: everything is about them, and what is good for them is good for everyone else. Some honestly can't differentiate between their needs and the needs of others—even children.

Victoria, a twelve-year-old, has never met her biological mother. She lives with her father Jim, a high-functioning BP, and Jim's longtime live-in girlfriend, Sally. Sally has been taking care of Victoria for ten years and the two of them have a close relationship—Victoria even calls her Mom. But Jim wants marriage and Sally doesn't. So when he met a woman who was marriage-minded, he decided to break up with Sally.

Jim, wanting his new wife to be Victoria's "mother," told Sally and Victoria they could not see each other anymore—even just to visit. Victoria began doing poorly at school and started having fights with her father and stepmother, while Sally was emotionally devastated. What would you do if you were Sally?

A. Accept Jim's decision. He is the father and it's his decision.

B. I wouldn't try to reason with anyone so stupid as Jim, who thinks you can turn a kid's feelings on and off like a faucet. I would sneak around and see Victoria when I could get a chance, like after school, so I could avoid dealing with Jim altogether.

C. I would write to Jim and try to explain how important I am to Victoria. Once he really understands, he'll probably change his mind.

D. I would do C, and if that didn't change his decision I would find a lawyer who could tell me if I had any legal rights to see Victoria.

Heads I Win, Tails You Lose, or No-Win Situations

This is the classic situation in which you're damned if you do and damned if you don't. Whatever the non-BP does, it will be incorrect. The "fault" of the non-BP is what this game is about, not the actual task or request.

The classic no-win situation is a threat of suicide followed by the words, "If you love me, don't tell anyone." Other no-win situations are more subtle.

Miranda: *No matter what I do, I just can't please my stepson Jerry. If we let him live at home, he accuses us of "controlling him." If we ask him to get his own apartment, he says we're "abandoning him." If I do his laundry, he says I am treating him like a child who can't be trusted to separate the colors and whites. If I leave his clothes for him to wash, he complains I don't think of him as a "real" member of the family. If I agree with him when he complains about his mother, he "gets" me for "belittling" her. If I say nothing, I'm not supporting him. When I tell this to his father he just shrugs his shoulders and says he's always been that way.*

A. If I were Miranda I would just do what Jerry wants and keep the peace.

B. I'll yell louder at him than he ever could at me. I'm not afraid of a fight. Then I would complain about the way he does things and find out a way to get back at him. Anyone like that has got to be crazy and I wouldn't put up with it.

C. I'd sit down with him and calmly and rationally explain his inconsistent behavior and its unfairness. He has to be able to see that this inconsistency is confusing and causes problems for everyone.

D. Clearly Jerry is inconsistent and doesn't make sense—which is typical for BPs. It's a good example of the "no-win" game, which often has nothing to do with the matter being discussed. Since I'm not going to be able to change him, I've got to take care of myself by constantly reminding myself that it's his problem, not mine, and setting personal limits and observing them.

Keep Your Distance a Little Closer

This is one of the most confusing, indecipherable patterns for non-BPs to understand. BPs feel the need for closeness and love to survive. But that is a scary thought because they feel worthless and are afraid others will find out. Keeping the mask up is hard work. BPs also feel engulfed when people become too close, partly because their sense of self is weak.

Since fear of abandonment is a central issue for the BP, the need for closeness soon kicks in. So she moves closer toward you. But then the pendulum swings and the fear of engulfment creeps in again. The BP's revolving emotions cloud her ability to put herself in another person's place and see things from your point of view. So when she needs you, she's not thinking about the fact that ten minutes ago she was threatening divorce.

Following are two examples of this behavior.

Ken: *This pattern happens in many ways. My girlfriend Amy will tell me I have to meet her at a certain time on the dot and she will show up an hour late. One night we have great sex; the next night she can't bear for me to touch her. We're on the telephone and Amy wants to break up, but by the end of the call she's planning a date for the next night. She says she loves me, then takes it back later, saying she thinks she may need to meet more men before "settling down." We constantly break up and get back together. I never know where we are from day to day. Will something I say set her off, or will she toss it off with a laugh?*

A. I can't force anyone to want to be with me, so if I were Ken I would just be together when I could and probably accept it when Amy didn't want me around.

B. Some people are like that. There's nothing much you can do.

C. Why this man is in this "relationship" I don't know. Is he a masochist? Amy is crazy and trying to make him crazy, too. Get out!

D. I would document this behavior and all Amy's contradictions and show her how this doesn't make any sense. She's smart—just not aware of what she's doing. Once she is, she'll probably stop this.

Marian: *I just can't figure out our teenage daughter, Heather. She is so moody, abusive, violent, and destructive that when she ran away, we felt guiltily relieved. She ended up at a friend's house, and the friend's parents said Heather could stay there for a week while things calmed down. She called me at work three days in a row, saying she was returning my messages and demanding to know why I kept calling her. But the truth was, I hadn't called her at all.*

A. If I were Marian, I'd feel guilty because I should have called Heather. What kind of mother lets her kid go live with someone else? I'd talk to her as long as she wanted.

B. If I were the mom, I'd be thinking, "Why does this child do this to me? How am I supposed to be able to do my job when she keeps calling and demanding my attention?" I'd tell Heather that if she doesn't start shaping up and following the rules, she can forget about coming home.

C. Heather's behavior doesn't make sense to me. If her mom's really the most worthless mother on the planet, why is she trying to talk to her all the time? Marian needs to tell the daughter she's not being logical.

Verbal Abuse: "I'm Saying This to Make You a Better Person"

Although most BPs do not intend to be verbally or emotionally abusive, their feelings cause them to act in ways that can feel like abuse to those around them.

What follows are some forms of emotional abuse outlined by author Beverly Engel (1990). If they apply to you, write an example or two in your notebook about how the activity takes place in your life. This will help you understand the material and retain it. After you're done, we will resume the Action Steps.

Domination. The person resorts to threats to get his own way.

Verbal assaults. This includes reprimanding, humiliating, criticizing, name-calling, screaming, threatening, excessive blaming, and using sarcasm in a cutting way. It also involves exaggerating other people's faults and making fun of them in front of others. Over time, this type of abuse erodes self-confidence and self-worth.

Abusive expectations. The other person makes unreasonable demands and expects that you will be her first priority—no matter what. This includes denouncing your own needs for attention and support.

Unpredictable responses. This includes drastic mood changes or sudden emotional outbursts—part of the definition of BPD. Living with someone like this is extremely anxiety-provoking. You may feel frightened, unsettled, and off-balance. This hypervigilance (constantly feeling "jumpy" and on guard against potential attacks) can even lead to physical illness.

Gaslighting. This involves denying a person's perceptions of events and conversations, especially those they know to be true.

Constant chaos. Deliberately starting arguments, creating drama, and being in constant conflict with others.

> **Roger:** *When our son Jake was in kindergarten, the teachers would tell me he had difficulty relating to the other children and didn't seem to get along with them at all. By grade school he had been in trouble several times, caught roaming the halls, stealing, lying, and so forth. In junior high, things got worse. He was totally out of control. At this point we put him into therapy. He would slam doors, call me names, say disrespectful things to his mother, call his younger sister "stupid," disregard punishment, and stay out late. He clearly thought I was the worst father that ever existed. Now that he's over eighteen, he's still seething and barely making it financially with his job*

as a bouncer for a bar. He has toned down a bit since he is always asking for money from us, but when he gets drunk he still says very hurtful things.

A. I wouldn't call this abuse. Abuse needs to be physical or sexual. Jake is just a person who has problems.

B. I would not tolerate that crap from my kid. I would tell Jake to get lost until he stopped all this behavior, and if he didn't I would consider the relationship finished.

C. I would try to logically explain what's happening and how this behavior affects me. If Jake is at all a decent person, he will change what he's doing.

D. Rather than trying to parcel out blame and such, if I were the father I would set personal limits. Jake and I could be together when he's non-abusive. But when he gets abusive, I would walk away or ask Jake to leave. No one deserves to be emotionally abused.

Now, count your number of A answers, B answers, and so forth. Record the number below.

Total number of "A" answers _____

Total number of "B" answers _____

Total number of "C" answers _____

Total number of "D" answers _____

This non-scientific Action Step helps you understand how you usually respond to typical BPD behaviors. *Becoming aware of this is just as important as understanding the BP's actions.* After all, you control 50 percent of the relationship.

While there are actually myriad responses, there are four basic ways of responding, as outlined here. You can alter your natural response. What's important is to honor your integrity—your firm adherence to your own values. You must also understand the long-term and short-term consequences of your actions. What is easiest in the short term—giving in to the BP's desires—is not necessarily the best answer in the long term because it damages the relationship and lessens your self-respect. Now let's look at what your answers mean:

Mostly "A" answers. This is a measure of what I'll call the "doormat" response. You probably don't like to challenge anyone, or have learned that doing so only seems to make things worse. This almost non-response is easy in the short-term because it avoids confrontation. But the long-term consequences of enduring abusive behavior can make you feel isolated, depressed, guilty, helpless, and hopeless. The longer you remain in this kind of relationship, the more you will probably become accustomed to the abuse. Eventually, you may forget that "normal" relationships allow both parties to have opinions, and both people should be willing to compromise for the sake of the relationship. In addition, if you have children, modeling "victim" behavior puts them at risk for getting into these types of relationships. For this reason alone, I would recommend that you read the rest of this workbook and learn more effective ways of responding. In sum, your challenge is to assert yourself, develop more confidence in your perceptions, and act in your own and your children's best long-term interest.

Mostly "B" answers. This is what I term the "angry" response. Even if you are not with the BP anymore, your anger may remain and could be touching other parts of your life. You may find yourself getting angry at family members, complete strangers, and situations you can't control. Unlike some people, you recognize emotional abuse. BPs can elicit strong negative emotions in all types of people. But instead of working through it, you may be nursing it and driving others away with unexpressed anger, grief, or other strong emotions. It could be affecting your job and relationships with friends and family, as well as interfering with your ability to let go and be happy.

Aside from dealing with your anger, your challenge is to look at yourself logically instead of putting false demands on yourself. For instance:

* You are not God. (My deepest apologies if God happens to be reading this.)

* You are not Superman or Superwoman.

Everyone has weaknesses, yourself and people with Superpowers included. Your ability to control situations is not the measure of your worth as a human being.

Mostly "C" answers. I call this the bargaining response. I've seen it mostly in people who are highly intelligent or who work in engineering or other scientific fields. A lot of borderline behavior does not "compute," and you may try again and again to reason with the BP or try to think of a rational way out of this situation. But it's like trying to run a Mac program on a PC. It won't work.

Remember, even though you can't look at BPD though a microscope, the BP in your life has a brain disorder. She is triggered by a variety of situations, and is highly ambivalent about a number of things. There are even biological reasons why a person in a highly emotional state may not be able to respond logically. So in this case, what is *logical* is to expect the BP to be *illogical*.

To become convinced of this, you may wish to recount all the times you've tried to explain yourself and the situation and record how well it worked. (If you don't remember, log each discussion/argument in your notebook. The log will help you measure what is actually happening without emotions clouding the results. You may also discover what phrases *do* help.)

Your challenge is to learn to accept situations in which your kind of logic does not prevail and BP logic reigns, and to learn new ways to communicate with the BP (I will cover some techniques in a later chapter). It may help to remember that just as people who have had a stroke may have trouble speaking, BPs may have trouble reasoning when they are highly excited. Now *that's* logical.

Mostly "D" answers. Although you can't change the BP, if you mainly answered "D" you are doing well in trying to set personal limits, recognizing what you can and cannot change, and responding in a way that takes care of your own feelings without letting the BP control your life directly or indirectly. The rest of this workbook will help you learn more skills like these.

📖 Action Step 13: Match That Dynamic

The statements on the left describe a type of BP/non-BP interaction; the right side a type of BP pattern. They are currently not aligned. Match each interaction on the left with the pattern on the right, and write them down in your notebook. In this example, there is only one correct answer to each item, and each item can be used only once. The answers are at the end of this chapter.

Interactions	Patterns
1. The BP: "I'm a man. I *need* to have sex every day even if you are tired and want to go to sleep."	A. Projection
2. The BP: "This is my husband Jerry—he'll forget your name in a few minutes, but I'll give it to him anyway. Jerry, this is Gail G=A=I=L. Got it?"	B. Everything is your fault
3. The BP: "I do not have BPD, Mr. Psychiatrist. If anyone has BPD, it's you! And I am not angry, you are!"	C. No-win situations
4. The BP: "I never hit you or intimidated you when we were kids. You just fell down a lot because you were clumsy. And I don't care if Mom and Dad said they saw me doing it. They're getting old and don't remember things very well."	D. Keep your distance a little closer
5. The non-BP is sitting quietly watching TV. The BP comes up and out of nowhere starts screaming abusive comments about something the non-BP knows nothing about.	E. Verbal abuse-domination
6. The BP: "If you tell Mom I went out and partied last night, I'll rip your room apart."	F. Verbal abuse–verbal assaults
7. The BP creates chaos at a restaurant when the cook forgets not to put mayonnaise on his sandwich. He is so loud, everyone in the restaurant looks over to see what the commotion is about.	G. Verbal abuse–abusive expectations
8. The non-BP: "We made love last night and it was wonderful. She told me to meet her here at exactly 11 A.M. and it's already noon. Why does something like this always happen when things are going well?"	H. Verbal abuse–unpredictable responses
9. The BP: "I feel like killing myself. But if you tell anyone or try to help me, I'll hate you."	I. Verbal abuse–gaslighting
10. The BP: "If I hadn't given birth to you, I could have pursued my dream of becoming an artist."	J. Verbal abuse–constant chaos

Real Life BP/Non-BP Interactions

As I said in the first chapter, an intellectual understanding of BPD is not the most troublesome part of improving the relationship. The real challenge lies in understanding BPD on an emotional level and applying it to your own life. On top of that, conversations can go so quickly that you must do several things at once:

1. Listen to what the BP is saying and identify the cognitive distortions;

2. Cope with your own emotions by reminding yourself that the disorder is affecting the situation and that you have many other choices of how to react;

3. Decide how to respond in a way that calms things down, keeps your integrity intact, and models good behavior for any children involved.

Accomplishing these three tasks almost simultaneously is not easy. If they were an event in the Olympics, they would rival the triple jumps in figure skating. But like all skills, you can learn how to do this one step at a time. One way to help you do this is to take a real-life situation, dissect what is happening, and determine the best way to respond. The next Action Step will help you do this.

📖 Action Step 14:
Identify BP/Non-BP Patterns

Read this excerpt from Rachel Reiland's book, *I'm Not Supposed to Be Here: My Recovery from Borderline Personality Disorder* (2002). Then do the exercises that follow.

The house was a complete disaster. Toys were strewn all over the floor, disposable diapers overflowed the trash can. Saltines lay smashed on the milk-spill-stained hardwood floor. Overloaded ashtrays, never emptied enough, spilled ashes on every tabletop. Fast-food wrappers were everywhere—from McDonald's, Wendy's, Taco Bell. God, I should get to this. I'm home. What kind of a mother am I? How can we afford all this fast food—much less what it must be doing to us? What in the hell am I doing here?

Picking up an armful of clothes, I headed for the steps. Damned drafty old house—two years after closing, it was still half-done, with no money to finish it. Gaping holes in the staircase waited for the quarter-round that never seemed to get put up—or couldn't we afford that, either? Eyeing the antique oak ball we'd put on the stair rail, visions of Jimmy Stewart rushed through my mind and I wished it weren't so well attached so I could pull it off or slam it down against the wall. But I had news for Jimmy—it was anything but "a wonderful life." It was a trap. Finally, the injustice of all the talent I was supposed to have but never deserved was catching up with me. I was broke. Disheveled. A three-year-old and an infant were still nursing the life right out of me, long after being weaned. They were napping. It was quiet. I was lonely and restless. I headed for the telephone.

"Um, is Tom there?"

"Please hold and I'll see if he's still here right now, Rachel."

God, how I hated that secretary—the way she spit out my name, the way she'd always keep me on hold forever and toy with me like Tom might not be there, even though she knew damned well that he was. She was always mocking me. I could just see her there at the switchboard, all made-up, wearing one of those damned designer suits that must have consumed half her salary. She was a goddamned secretary, no less, who thought she was CEO. And I envied her. Bitch.

"This is Tom."

"Hi, Tom . . ."

Dead silence. Why in the hell had I called, anyway? God, I was pathetic.

"Rachel? Are you there?"

"Yes, I'm here."

"Well, what do you want, hon? I'm kind of busy here, I've got a presentation in a half hour."

"Oh . . ."

"Is something wrong?"

"I hate this house, Tom. I just hate it. It's a hellhole. The kids are napping, but I just don't feel like cleaning it."

"Then don't clean it. Take a nap yourself. I can help you with it when I get home."

"When are you coming home?"

"I dunno. I have a whole life [insurance] presentation in a half hour and then I got a call from my annuities ad—I thought I'd go over there at about five."

"Then you won't be home until six or seven!"

"I know, but I haven't gotten a lot done lately . . ."

"And it's my fault, isn't it?"

"I didn't say it's your fault, honey. It's just that—well, I've got to get some stuff done."

I began to twist the phone cord around my finger, tempted to do so around my neck.

"I'm a real pain in the ass, aren't I? You're pissed, aren't you?"

Tom tried to keep his patience, but I could still hear him sigh.

"Please, Rachel. I've got to make a living."

"Like, I don't do anything around here? Is that it? Like I'm some kind of stupid housewife that just sits around here and doesn't do a goddamned thing? Is that what you're getting at?"

Another sigh.

"Okay. Look, sweetheart. I've got to do this presentation this afternoon because it's too late to cancel. But I'll see if I can reschedule the annuity guy for tomorrow. I'll be home by four and I'll help you clean up the house."

"No, no, no!"

I was beginning to cry.

"What now?"

"God, Tom. I'm such an idiot! Such a baby! I don't do a damned thing around this house, and here I am, wanting you to help me clean. I must make you sick!"

"You don't make me sick, sweetheart. Okay? You don't. Look—I'm really sorry but I've got to go—"

The tears reached full-strength. The cry became a moan that turned to piercing screams. Why in the hell can't I control myself? The man has to make a living! He's such a good guy, he doesn't deserve me—no one deserves to have to put up with me! Goddamnit, why can't I stop crying? But I couldn't—the piercing screams overwhelmed me, took me over, possessed me.

"Rachel? Rachel? Please calm down. Please! Come on, you're gonna wake up the kids, the neighbors are gonna wonder what in the hell is going on. Rachel?"

"Fuck you! Is that all you give a shit about, what the fucking neighbors think? Fuck you, then. I don't need you home. I don't want you home. Let this fucking house rot for all I care, let the fucking kids starve. I don't give a shit. And I don't need your shit!"

"Rachel, listen to me. I'm canceling the whole life appointment, I'll be home in a few minutes. Okay?"

"You must really hate me," I sobbed. "You really hate me, don't you?"

"No, sweetheart," he sighed audibly. "I don't hate you."

Now, please reread the following parts of the story and circle which of the two BPD behaviors or interactions (a or b) they best exemplify.

1. *What kind of a mother am I? . . . What in the hell am I doing here?*

These two sentences indicate:

    a. Hopelessness, despair and distorted and enlarged errors

    b. A pattern of unstable relationships

2. *I had news for Jimmy—it was anything but "a wonderful life." It was a trap. Finally, the injustice of all the talent I was supposed to have but never deserved was catching up with me. I was broke. Disheveled. A three-year-old and an infant were still nursing the life right out of me, long after being weaned. They were napping. It was quiet. I was lonely and restless. I headed for the telephone.*

This section could indicate:

    a. Splitting

    b. Feelings of emptiness

3. Rachel: *"Um, is Tom there?"*
Secretary: *"Please hold and I'll see if he's still here right now, Rachel." God, how I hated that secretary—the way she spit out my name, the way she'd always keep me on hold forever and toy with me like Tom might not be there, even though she knew damned well that he was. . . . Bitch.*

From what you know, Rachel seems to dislike the secretary because:

    a. The secretary is verbally abusive.

    b. Rachel is projecting her low self-worth onto the secretary, assuming the secretary doesn't like her when Rachel really doesn't like herself.

4. Rachel: *"Then you won't be home until six or seven!"* Tom: *"I know, but I haven't gotten a lot done lately . . ."* Rachel: *"And it's my fault, isn't it?"* Tom: *"I didn't say it's your fault, honey. It's just that—well, I've got to get some stuff done."* I began to twist the phone cord around my finger, tempted to do so around my neck. Rachel: *"I'm a real pain in the ass, aren't I? You're pissed, aren't you?"* Tom tried to keep his patience, but I could still hear him sigh. *"Please, Rachel. I've got to make a living."*

Pick the answer that you think sums up this section:

    a. Tom is trying to explain his situation logically to Rachel, but this doesn't seem to be affecting her unhappiness. BPs don't usually respond to logic when their emotions are high.

    b. This is an example of one of *DSM-IV*'s criteria for BPD: identity disturbance.

5. Tom: *"Please, Rachel. I've got to make a living."* Rachel: *"Like, I don't do anything around here? Is that it? Like I'm some kind of stupid housewife that just sits around here and doesn't do a goddamned thing? Is that what you're getting at?"*

    a. Rachel believes she isn't worth much, but rather than face her own feelings of worthlessness, she instead accuses Tom of seeing her as worthless. This is projection on Rachel's part.

    b. Tom has a problem with Rachel's housekeeping.

6. Tom: *Another sigh. "Okay. Look, sweetheart. I've got to do this presentation this afternoon because it's too late to cancel. But I'll see if I can reschedule the annuity guy for tomorrow. I'll be home by four and I'll help you clean up the house."*

    a. Tom is trying to compromise: making one of his commitments and rescheduling another. This is a successful way to cope with Rachel's problems.

    b. Tom is trying to compromise: making one of his commitments and rescheduling another. There is a risk, though, that since this was a successful way to get Tom's attention, Rachel will call him another day and ask him to cancel appointments and come home early. If that gets to be a habit, their income could suffer and Rachel may not try to use her own inner resources to soothe herself.

7. *"No, no, no!"* I was beginning to cry. Tom: *"What now?"* Rachel: *"God, Tom. I'm such an idiot! Such a baby! I don't do a damned thing around this house, and*

here I am, wanting you to help me clean. I must make you sick!" Tom: *"You don't make me sick, sweetheart. Okay? You don't. Look—I'm really sorry but I've got to go—"* *The tears reached full-strength. The cry became a moan that turned to piercing screams . . . that overwhelmed me, took me over, possessed me.*

    a. Rachel is simply being manipulative, trying to hurt someone else to get her own way.

    b. This is an example of the *DSM-IV* BP trait number 6: affective instability (unstable moods that can do a 180-degree swing in seconds, minutes, or hours).

8. Tom: *"Rachel? Rachel? Please calm down. Please! Come on, you're gonna wake up the kids, the neighbors are gonna wonder what in the hell is going on. Rachel?"* Rachel: *"Fuck you! Is that all you give a shit about, what the fucking neighbors think? Fuck you, then. I don't want you home. . . . And I don't need your shit!"*

    a. This is probably part of the come here–go away abandonment/engulfment dynamic. It also demonstrates *DSM-IV* BP trait number eight, inappropriate, intense anger.

    b. When Rachel says she doesn't want Tom home, she is showing high-functioning independence.

9. Tom: *"Rachel, listen to me. I'm canceling the whole life appointment. I'll be home in a few minutes. Okay?"* Rachel: *"You must really hate me,"* I sobbed. *"You really hate me, don't you?"* *"*Tom: *"No, sweetheart,"* he sighed audibly. *"I don't hate you."*

    a. Throughout this conversation, Rachel wants to be able to control herself, but there is no evidence that she understands why she feels the way she does or what to do about it.

    b. Tom could have talked Rachel out of her mood if he just knew what to say.

In the last three chapters I've explained BPD in a variety of ways, enlightened you about some BPD behavior and discussed interactions between BPs and those people who care about them. In the next chapter, I'll look at how BPD behavior affects you, your outlook on life, and your feelings about yourself.

Answers to Action Step 13:

1. G

2. F

3. A

4. I

5. H

6. E

7. J

8. D

9. C

10. B

Answers to Action Step 14:

1. A

2. B

3. B

4. A

5. A

6. B

7. B

8. A

9. B

Chapter 6

Beyond Denial: Accepting
What You Cannot Change
(And Changing What You Can)

I thought that if I worked harder, more often, kept the house a bit cleaner, surely he would love me. But he didn't. Giving up hope saved my life.

—Charles, a non-BP

Change is difficult, but it is possible. One important thing you need to know, though, is that change is even harder for the BP than it is for you. As with alcoholism, a common symptom of Borderline Personality Disorder among acting-out, high-functioning BPs is denial. An alcoholic will drink until he blacks out every night and proclaim he is "fine"; a person who shows all nine BPD traits may deny the disorder's existence in himself, but curiously find it in many other people in his life.

But the BP isn't the only one in denial. While some family members and friends are relieved to discover that this condition has a diagnosis, some think of the disorder as a temporary setback that will disappear with time, with more love or the right kind of loving, or by some other means that doesn't involve time, hard work in therapy, and perhaps medication. Many non-BPs try to change the BP—or they try to change themselves to meet the BP's ever-changing demands. But when they complete their task and like Dorothy bring back the broomstick of the Wicked Witch, the great and powerful Oz always has another impossible task to be fulfilled. In this case, he will deny he ever asked for the broomstick in the first place.

Relationship Outcomes

If someone you love has BPD, you may find that one of the following will happen after you understand the role BPD plays in the BP's behavior.

* You deny that BPD is a problem and do nothing. The status quo reigns.

* The BP denies that BPD is a problem. The status quo reigns, except that you go nuts trying to change him.

* You accept the person as she is and allow the disorder to claim the happiness in your life as well as the BP's.

* You accept the person as he is, but protect yourself with the techniques in this workbook, *SWOE*, or other books. You may work with a therapist.

* You and/or the BP acknowledge the existence of BPD and learn all about it on an intellectual level. Change may or may not result.

* The BP learns enough about BPD to accuse you of having it, and/or you concentrate on the BP's disorder to avoid looking at your own issues, such as codependency.

* The BP acknowledges there is a problem, but does very little to accomplish lasting change. He may stay with an inexperienced therapist who will not dig very deep, who is unfamiliar with the disorder, or who can be easily conned.

* The BP will acknowledge she has a problem and will work hard with a good psychiatric staff to overcome the disorder—a process that may take

two or three years. The non-BP hopefully learns ways in which he can reinforce therapy and confront his own issues, if appropriate.

Of course, everyone wants an immediate awakening, a miracle cure such as a pill or therapy that will work overnight and turn everything all around. I haven't personally seen such a miracle, but I have seen non-BPs witness their children being emotionally abused while the other parent waits for this miracle to happen.

Non-BP's, being human, want the BP to understand them, validate their experiences, apologize, empathize, and stop borderline behaviors that threaten the relationship. People with BPD may or may not ask, but most of them want their friends and family members to understand their pain, fulfill their needs, and assuage their feelings of emptiness, worthlessness, pain, and other painful borderline feelings.

No matter how much you love someone, you cannot make them love themselves and make the best choices for themselves. This is one of the hardest things for both non-BPs and borderlines to accept. The person with the disorder must, with help from a clinician, support groups, and other resources, conquer her own demons.

But change is not easy for either the non-BP or the BP. And in order for everything to get better, non-BPs need to change as well—they can't just put that task on the BP. Each person is 100 percent responsible for their 50 percent of the relationship.

You've probably asked yourself, "Will the BP in my life take responsibility for any of his behavior, and if so, how much?" But you also need to know, "Am I able and willing to implement the suggestions in this workbook, and to what extent?" You may not be able to answer these questions now, but they are at the heart of your primary concerns: Are you going to get your needs met in this relationship? Will you feel safe? And will you ever be on the receiving end of courtesy and respect?

📖 Action Step 20:
Past Efforts to Change the BP

You know by now—at least on a rational level—that you can't change anyone but yourself. But if you're like most people living with a BP, a part of you may still feel responsible for changing someone else. That feeling is normal. So let's take a look at your efforts to change the BP in your life and see how they've worked out.

Below, you'll find three blank columns with different headings. On the left, make a list of everything you asked the BP to change about herself, from small to large. Next to this list, write down all the things you did to motivate the BP to change, in each case. Include things like nagging, giving rewards, punishments, and ultimatums—whatever you tried. Then, on the right, write down the results of your efforts. Did these behavior change? If so, for how long? Were there any unexpected results? If the BP wanted to change a trait about themselves, was there a different result? Think carefully about whether you changed the BP or whether the BP agreed with you and decided to change himself.

Change Wanted	Methods Tried	Results
_____	_____	_____
_____	_____	_____
_____	_____	_____
_____	_____	_____
_____	_____	_____
_____	_____	_____
_____	_____	_____
_____	_____	_____

If you are like most non-BPs—especially those who have chosen their relationship with the borderline—you feel responsible for "fixing" or "rescuing" the BP from their own self-defeating habits and ways of thinking. The benefit of this belief is that it gives you a sense of control. But it's an illusion. You can't fundamentally change anyone. You can show the BP a path and talk about the benefits of that path, you can manipulate the BP for a short time through rewards and punishments (especially if the BP is a child), but as soon as you stop the reward or punishment, the BP's old, familiar ways of thinking and behaving will return. This next Action Step will help you feel that.

📖 Action Step 21: A Change Experiment

Experiment 1. Write the following phrase with your non-dominant hand (your left hand if you are right-handed and you right hand if you are left-handed, or if you are ambidextrous, write with a pencil between your toes): "I am learning a new skill and I should be able to do it perfectly the first time. There is no excuse for sloppiness or imperfection."

1. Did the fact that you didn't previously *need* to know how to write with your non-dominant hand affect your attitude, success, or willingness to try this experiment? _____

2. Think about the content of what you wrote. Did you believe it before the Action Step? During? After? _____

James Paul Shirley got the idea for this Action Step from a gifted fencing coach who was also a clinical psychologist. After many weeks of making them practice the same dry, repetitive fencing movements until they became totally boring and discouraging, the coach asked the students do the same moves left-handed. It was only then that they had an "Aha!" experience and realized how much progress they had made.

In all likelihood, you will reach a time when you are trying your best to use the techniques in this workbook and you will feel as if you've gotten nowhere. That's the time to recall this Action Step. Learning takes time, and you need to be patient with yourself while you are learning and growing.

Experiment 2. Pick a habit you want to change, something that is a goal of yours that gives you a direct benefit, such as starting an Action Step program, losing weight, spending more time with your kids, etc. Make the goal reasonable and within reach. If you succeed, what will the benefits be? Write these benefits down and refer to them throughout the week. _____

_____

_____

Spend one week working hard on your goal and then answer these questions:

1. What habit did you choose to change? _____

_____

2. Did you make it through the week? If not, how long were you able to keep it up? _____

_____

3. Was it hard to remember to make this change? _____

_____

4. Did it feel less strange as the week progressed? _____

_____

5. If you continued this experiment for another week or two, do you suppose it would become easier? Would you become better at it? _____

_____

6. Did the fact that this was something you wanted and you chose affect your attitude, success, or willingness to try this experiment? _____

_____

This Action Step should have reinforced that change is difficult, especially if it's something you have to think about and keep in the forefront of your mind most of the time. Additionally, if you're not motivated to change, there is little chance of success. Success depends upon keeping the benefits of the change at the top of your mind.

If changing something about yourself that you want to change is difficult, imagine how difficult it is for people with a personality disorder to change—even if they want to. And if they don't want to—if the coping mechanism seems to be working for them—there is almost no chance they will change, unless they're manipulated into it by an ultimatum. Ultimatums and other manipulative devices rarely create lasting change, however. A person needs personal skills, encouragement, intrinsic or extrinsic rewards, necessary skills, and something to put in place of the thing that is lost. This is one reason why professional help is so necessary for people with BPD. Losing a coping mechanism without something to put in its place is very frightening.

Identity Issues

Change is especially difficult if it changes our self-definition. Eva, for example, has had a difficult life. Her parents divorced when she was an infant, she was molested when she was ten, she has lived in poverty, and many members of her extended family have been killed. As much as Eva would like to change some of the dysfunctional ways she copes, she wonders who she would be without the pain she has been carrying around most of her life. That pain has defined her. It has made her who she is. Once you take that away, what is left? Such feelings need to be discussed with a mental health professional. With help, Eva can hopefully become the person she was meant to be while giving up mourning for the things she never had and the things she had and lost.

Borderline Behavior Is Not about You

Your BP's capacity or desire to change is not in your control. You have to accept the fact that seeking treatment is entirely his decision. You can tell him how his actions and words make you feel and suggest solutions. But what he does with that information is out of your hands.

What *is* in your hands are your emotional reactions to the BP's borderline behaviors. There is a popular saying posted in many workplaces: A crisis on your part does not necessarily mean a crisis on my part.

If the BP in your life is having a crisis because he doesn't agree with the personal limit you've set, you don't have to respond to his complaints, protests, rages, or limit-testing. You can simply reiterate your limit and act confidently. For example, when a sick BP wanted me to care for him, I refused to be yelled at and quietly said I would leave if the behavior continued. It stopped right away.

Detaching with Love

"Detach with Love" should be your motto. You need to keep your life from being a series of BPD-related crises. The message to your BP is: "I care about you, but I recognize that you must make your own choices in life. I can love you, but I can't live your life for you. I can point you in the right direction, but I can't push you down the path."

The BP is responsible for the crises she creates. It is a BPD trait to create dramas, consciously or unconsciously. You can make those emotional dramas your problem, or you can let the BP handle them as best she can (given the appropriateness of the situation and the age of the BP).

If you take responsibility for the BP's chaos, you risk reinforcing that behavior and causing yourself a lot of grief. If you let the BP handle her own problems, it's more likely that she'll learn how to take care of things herself or avoid dramas altogether.

Letting Go of the BP's Problems

The first step in detaching with love is to let go of problems that do not really involve you. Naturally, the BP will try to make you responsible either directly ("This is your fault!") or indirectly (blaming you for not getting her college application forms when she forgot to get them and therefore missed her deadline).

Once you learn to emotionally let go of what you *can't* control and stop letting the BP cast you as the villain of his dramas, you'll be able express love and concern while assuring the BP he can handle the dilemma by himself. If you keep doing this consistently, the BP will realize that he doesn't have to create tests to prove you love him. And when you stop covering up mistakes, cleaning up messes, and taking responsibility for his problems, he can begin to grow emotionally and begin to take real responsibility for himself.

Detaching with love starts with you. You must truly convince yourself that you are not responsible for another person's disorder or recovery from it—even if that person is your child. Naturally if the BP is under eighteen, you will have to use common sense to decide what actions to take. But no matter how old the BP is, you do not have to let the BP see you get flustered, upset, or lose control. The calmer you are and the more you can let him take responsibility, the more you will reinforce that he is capable of taking care of the problem himself.

Remember: It's Detaching "With Love"

It's important to remember the "with love" part. Detaching with love is not a matter of judging others, controlling their actions, or implying approval or disapproval. If the world were a big hardware store and someone came up to you looking for the auto parts section, you might say, "I'm sorry, but I'm not the sales clerk. I don't know where the auto parts are, but perhaps someone can help you at the customer service counter." This is a good example of detaching with love. It's not snapping, "Do you see me wearing a uniform? No? Then leave me alone!"

📖 Action Step 22, Part One: Learning to Detach with Love

James Paul Shirley first learned this Action Step at a retreat intended to nurture spiritual development. It can serve as a powerful catalyst to help individuals free themselves from old entrenched patterns of thinking, feeling, and behaving. He came up with three different versions. Use whichever one you like best. Feel free to rephrase the wording to make the exercise right for you.

Think of the first name of the person from whom you would like to detach. Use the person's first name, even if the BP is one of your parents. I will use the name "Joe" as an example. Now repeat the following sentence in one of the three formats. You may repeat it out loud, or say it silently to yourself.

Format 1: "I release Joe into God's care, and Joe releases me into God's care."

Format 2: "I release Joe to the Light, and Joe releases me to the Light."

Format 3: "I release Joe to his own highest good, and Joe releases me to my own highest good."

Take about twenty seconds to concentrate on this message, and repeat the sentence several times. Some people experience an immediate sensation of inner peacefulness. If you wish to, savor the message for longer than twenty seconds. Next, in the blanks below write down the first names of other people you need to detach from. Then, for each person, say each statement, wait for about twenty seconds, then repeat it.

_____   _____

_____   _____

_____   _____

_____   _____

_____   _____

📖 *Action Step 22, Part Two: Detachment Phrases*

Use phrases like those below to show you care but need to place the responsibility for the problem back where it belongs. Check off the statements and responses that seem most appropriate to your situation, and memorize them. The more you practice, the easier the responses will be to use. Since you know your own situation best, at the end write some other statements and possible responses like the ones given.

_____ The BP: "Where did you put my wallet?"

_____ The non-BP: "I don't know where you put it. Why don't you think about where you last used it and retrace your steps from there?"

_____ The BP (driving in a car): "It's your fault we're lost."

_____ The non-BP (passenger): "I don't feel at fault. Let's stop at the nearest gas station and you can ask for directions."

_____ The BP: "I can't do this. Would you do it for me?"

_____ The non-BP: "I understand it may seem overwhelming. If you break up the task into smaller pieces, it will look a whole lot more manageable."

_____ The BP: "There's no way I'm going to take responsibility for this! If you hadn't (done such and such), this never would have happened!"

_____ The non-BP: "I don't feel responsible, but either way, arguing is not going to solve this problem. Perhaps if you (do so such and such) this problem can be solved."

_____ The BP: "I can't do what I told you I'd do. Something else has come up."

_____ The non-BP: "I can see your dilemma. But you promised me you would do this last Tuesday, and I expect you to keep your promise."

_____ The BP: _____

_____ The non-BP: _____

_____ The BP: _____

_____ The non-BP: _____

New Skills Replace Older Ones

Once you decide to take control of your own life, your primary goal will be different. Instead of walking on eggshells trying to please the BP, you will walk on firm ground and try to please yourself. You too can replace old habits with new coping skills.

First you should concentrate on this thought:

Differences of opinion are all right, and everyone has a right to his own opinion, including both you and the BP. Since everything is black or white to the BP, you may have lost sight of this fact. But its ramifications are powerful. Both you and the BP have the right to hold your own opinions on everything, from the existence of God to how often the bathroom should be cleaned. This means that you don't have to make the BP believe your "truth," and you don't need to accept the BP's opinions as truth either. You can agree to disagree.

📖 Action Step 23:
It's Okay to Disagree

In this exercise, you're going to test the theory that it's okay to disagree. You will need to find a partner, preferably a friend who grew up in a family that allowed for dissenting opinions, someone who's comfortable with themselves and who they are. You can choose someone you don't know that well, but be sure to choose someone who is non-threatening.

Now, come up with a potentially controversial opinion about something—an opinion you really hold or one you just want to play with. Don't make it an opinion that some people put great emotional stock in (e.g., a religious belief) or something that is just impolite under the circumstances (the importance of fox hunting to the British upper class at a meeting of the People for the Ethical Treatment of Animals). Here are some sample phrases and a space to write in your own.

* "I think the Three Stooges are greatly underrated comic actors."

* "Golf is a boring sport."

* "You should always leave a tip for the waiter, even if the service is bad."

* "I think that George W. Bush will be heralded as one of our greatest presidents."

* "I've always thought there's just not enough sex and violence on television."

Now, try asserting one of these opinions when you're with your friend or acquaintance. A chance may come up spontaneously. Take note of how she reacts. If she gets huffy, just smile and say, "That's my opinion. What's yours?" If she laughs or says whatever is on her mind, relax. This is how things are supposed to happen. Next, try another statement—a harder one if the first one went well, a softer one if the first one did not.

The point of this Action Step was for you to feel comfortable giving a dissenting opinion among people who generally respect everyone's right to have their own opinion. Try this Action Step often, varying it every once in a while. For example, do something the BP in your life would never give you, approve of, or leave you time for. *Make* the time and do it with joy. Practice independent thinking and behaving as often as you can, even if it's choosing a different brand of ice cream. Keep track of your progress in your notebook. It should become easier and more fun over time.

📖 *Action Step 24:*
Your Mental (or Actual) Vacation

The best way to gain some clarity in your life is to take a mental—or physical, if possible—break away from your BP. I have seen it work miracles dozens of times: people stepping out of Oz and regaining their perspective on themselves and their situation. Whether your break is physical or mental, the point is not to think about your BP during this time, but simply to have fun with people who like and support you and do not easily take offense.

During this time, relax and forget about maintaining limits, speaking in exact ways, and walking on eggshells. Don't nurse any wounds, hold any grudges, or let sorrow spoil this time. You're taking a vacation away from issues and problems involving the BP.

I can't tell you exactly how to customize this for your life. But it is absolutely vital that you take a holiday away from the work associated with having someone in your life with BPD. (You are lucky that you can do this; the BP cannot escape himself.) What you do, of course, depends on the type of relationship you have and the particulars of your own situation.

The mother of a BP son talks about taking a "mental vacation": *I do a sport called endurance riding, which is going fifty miles on a horse. It's a team event, and you and the horse have to be in shape. During the ride, I have to be completely attuned to the horse—is it lame or dehydrated? Does it need a rest? I'm outside, in beautiful country I can't get to any other way. When I ride, I can't think about my borderline child at all. It is totally absorbing. The mental vacation keeps me sane.*

Here is how one man took an actual vacation from his borderline wife: *I went to a gathering of people with borderline spouses like me. For three days, we ate, laughed, talked, sat by a campfire, and shared stories. I didn't have to worry about walking on eggshells. No one blamed or criticized me for anything. I realized just how abnormal my life* *has become and what it is like to have fun again. Most of all, I felt validated because everyone there is going through the same thing. They really understood. That three days changed my life.*

Use your notebook to describe your activity and how you felt during or after it. Try this Action Step often and you will become more comfortable with it. Do it until you're positively, absolutely sure that the world doesn't end when you say or do something that displeases the great and powerful Oz, who, after all, is just a man behind a curtain.

Depending on your particular situation, it may be difficult to arrange this last Action Step. Do it anyway, even if you have to tell a white lie to get some time to yourself. People who live with someone with BPD soon becomes like a fish in water: they can't describe what their world is like because they have no other perspective. If you are concerned about the BP during this time, remember that it is healthy for two adults to be able to spend some time without each other's presence. If your BP is a minor child and is in therapy, ask her therapist about a short separation and obtain some advice specific to your circumstances.

📖 Action Step 25: Because I Say So!

This is another Action Step that will help you get in touch with who you are, what you want, what you like and don't like, and how you feel. The object is to make sure you voice *your* opinions, feelings, and so forth. Recite each of the statements out loud, filling in the blanks and ending each with "because I say so." Yes, you will feel dumb when you start. But by the end, fill your voice with the intensity and conviction of Martin Luther King standing amongst millions of people on the steps at the Lincoln Memorial shouting, "I have a dream!" At the end, come up with some of your own phrases. You still may feel silly. But do it anyway.

* The thing I like best about me is _____ , just because I say so!

* The world would be a better place if _____ , just because I say so!

* I think that everyone should _____ , just because I say so!

* If I won a million dollars, the first thing I would do is _____ , just because I say so!

* If I were president I would _____ , just because I say so!

* If we only got rid of _____ , the world would be
a better place, just because I say so!

* If I owned that TV network, they would have _____ ,
just because I say so!

* Some people think _____ about me, but it's not
true, just because I say so!

* _____ , just because I say so!

In Beverly Engel's book *Loving Him Without Losing You: Seven Empowering Strategies for Better Relationships* (2000), I found this quote by a woman named Liana Cordes: "I have listened to everyone else's truth and tried to make it mine. Now I am listening deep inside my own voice and I am softly, yet firmly, speaking my truth" (197). That's what this Action Step was about—finding your own voice and speaking your own truth. You have been listening to everyone else's truth— the BP's, your family, and friends—it's time to begin to listen to and trust the healthy voice inside yourself.

In the wonderful Mexican film *Like Water for Chocolate* (1992), set in the late 1800s, the mother, Elena, treats her youngest adult daughter, Tita, like a servant. She even refuses to let Tita marry, expecting her daughter to stay at home and take care of her until she dies of old age. Meanwhile, Mama Elena gives the two older sisters as much love as she can muster—and cruelly arranges the marriage of Tita's beloved to her eldest daughter, Rosura, commanding Tita to make the wedding cake and forbidding her to cry. Later in the film, Mama Elena is killed. Even then, she comes back as a ghost and haunts her Cinderella-like daughter with the same barbs and abuse she showered on her when she was living. Finally, the daughter gains strength and tells her abusive ghost mother that she hates her. She tells her to go away and to never come back, and that she will not accept her mother's abuse from the Beyond any longer. It works. When Tita speaks her truth—even to a ghost abuser—it banishes her.

Was Elena really a ghost, or did she represent Tita's own self-recriminations, the way people who have been abused continue to abuse themselves after the abuser is no longer there? It doesn't matter. What matters is that you have more power than you think you do. No one can get inside your mind and force you to accept abuse. Take care that you don't become your own abuser by putting yourself down, either out loud or in your mind.

Try looking at yourself the way the people who love you see you. Ask them to write it down for you, if you're comfortable with that. Then, write a letter to yourself about all the things you like about the new you. Let go of old scripts you don't need anymore. You are the screenwriter of your own life.

📖 *Action Step 26:*
Frankie Says Relax

One non-BP said it all when he made this remark. "We do what we can. Then we do the dishes." Yes, life does go on despite the problems in your relationship, the BP's painful feelings, and your ambivalence, worry, and chaos. This relaxation Action Step is a basic building block for some of the later Action Steps in this book. Paying attention to the feelings in your body is an important skill, and you will need to draw on it later. This exercise will work best if you record the script that follows and play it back to yourself.

Relaxation Exercise Instructions

Find a comfortable place to sit where you will not be disturbed for about twenty to thirty minutes. Sit up with your back straight, but not rigid. Keep your legs and ankles straight in front of you and uncrossed. Keeping your mind blank, close your eyes and picture a sky blue square against a fluffy white cloud. As thoughts drift in, just let them drift out. Yawn and stretch. Take a deep breath and hold it, then reach your arms out at an angle over your head so that they make the shape of the letter "Y." As you hold your arms up and out, clench both fists and flex your wrists. Relax and lower your hands to your lap. Take a slow, gently deep breath and let it out gradually. Repeat the yawn and stretch a second time, then a third. You may be starting to feel some loosening in your muscles.

Now pay attention to the various muscle groups in your body. Begin with your feet. Notice how they feel—warm or cool, tense or relaxed. Tense the muscles in your feet and hold that tension for three to five seconds, then relax. Move your attention up to the calves of your legs. Notice how they feel—warm or cool, tense or relaxed. Hold the muscles tight and for three to five seconds, then shake them out. Do the same with the rest of your body, including your thigh muscles, buttocks, your lower back and abdomen, chest and upper back area, both shoulders, neck, jaw, and forehead. Hold the tension for three to five seconds, then slowly relax them. Gradually take a few deep abdominal breaths (you'll see your stomach rise); let your breath out slowly. Imagine that the stiffness is leaving your body each time you exhale. You may be starting to feel warm and relaxed throughout your whole body. Enjoy the feeling. You deserve it. Deeply breathe again, and as you exhale let go of all the remaining tension in your whole body.

Your whole body is now entering a state of warm, deep relaxation. Keep breathing slowly and naturally, in and out, and keep your muscles loose. Now imagine that you are lying on a beach somewhere, soaking up the warm summer sun. You can hear the distant sounds of waves crashing against the shore in the background. You can even hear seagulls crying in the distance. You feel the warmth of the sunlight penetrating your body, and you enjoy the feeling it brings to your muscles and bones, even to the marrow inside your bones. You can visualize the golden rays of sunlight as they penetrate your body. The warm, soothing rays heal you from the inside out, calming and reenergizing every part that they touch.

Now pretend that you're growing lighter because you've released so much tension. You're drifting upward like a wisp of fog toward the sun's healing touch. The sunlight caresses your body and you feel calm and tender, without a care in the world. This is what you deserve, so enjoy it to the fullest.

Whenever you are ready, you may begin drifting slowly back down to the place where you sat at the beginning of this Action Step. Move slowly and lightly, like a cloud drifting down. Take a slow, deep breath and slowly let it out. As you come back, the calmness and healing light stays within you. Notice how your body feels against whatever you are sitting on; the sensations of pressure against your body. Savor the feeling and smell the clean air and feel the breeze touch your skin and soothe the muscles underneath. Notice the sounds around you.

Take another deep breath and release it slowly. Now you are fully back into the present, rested and reenergized. Stretch your arms up and out, taking another deep breath; stretch and yawn. Relax your arms and bring them back down into your lap. Look around you and notice where you are. You are fully back to your starting point, with the difference that you feel the healing inner light relaxing you from within.

One habit that non-BPs tend to fall into is forgetting about their own feelings. Although it is true that you need certain factual information to deal with BPD, you will also need the information that comes directly from your feelings. In chapter 8, for instance, you will learn how to recognize when you are being manipulated by fear, obligation, and guilt. One of your main tools for recognizing manipulation is simply noticing how your body feels at any given time. Sometimes your educated intellect will tell you the things you need to know about dealing with BPD, but at other times you cannot replace the information that comes only from your body. Once you know how your body feels when you are fully relaxed, you'll be able to detect any changes. Your body may even warn you of impending trouble before your brain does.

In this chapter, we started you on the path of self-determination with some examples of how you can assert yourself. In the next chapter, we will show you how to start treasuring the most important person in your life—you.

Chapter 7

Treasuring Yourself: Owning Your Own Reality

When we let ourselves be defined in our own minds by our worst moments instead of our best ones, we learn to think of ourselves as people who never get it right, rather than as capable people who make an occasional, thoroughly human mistake.

—Rabbi Harold Kushner

*A*s I write this chapter, a phenomenon of "reality-based" television shows has swept the country. I'll call one of the two favorites *I Eat Bugs for Money*. Several lucky contestants endure great physical hardships, including starvation, to win a million dollars. In the other one, which I'll call *Locked In with Losers*, people are being taped and broadcast on the Internet around the clock (even in the bathroom), locked in a house with twelve other strangers—some of whom they wouldn't sit next to on the subway—for the chance of winning $500,000.

The goal of each game is the same—to outlast everyone else and win the cash. But to do that, contestants must accomplish two opposing goals: first, get rid of their competition, and second, be well-liked enough to obtain the competition's winning vote.

Like all television, the shows have only one purpose: to draw an audience of people for advertisers. But as a writer of self-help books, I see them as fascinating sociology and psychology experiments. One day it hit me that, despite their different strategies, most of the winners on the shows had one thing in common: from the very beginning, they acted with the confidence and leadership of someone who had already won. Some of the winners even predicted at the outset they would outlast the competition.

Beliefs Create Your Reality

You might think that the winner's early confidence would convince other contestants to get rid of this contestant as quickly as possible. But the other contestants didn't, or couldn't. The winners—even the unlikable ones—seemed to have a presence that helped them win.

So what does this have to do with you? Everything. You may not be willing to eat bugs for money or be locked inside a house with a bunch of strangers. But the same principle applies: *The way you view yourself will compel others to treat you accordingly.* If you feel like you're a loser, you will come across as a loser and people may treat you that way. If you see yourself as a confident, worthy person (or do a good job of pretending you feel that way), people will sense it and treat you accordingly.

How Beliefs Create Reality

The way you view yourself is but one of your "realities"; every choice you make in life comes from a point of view you have learned over time—what other people, situations, and life events have taught you about yourself and your place in the world. All too often, non-BPs have come to the conclusion that they are undeserving, their choices are limited, and they are definitely not winners in the game of life. But as we grow up, we can learn to change that view.

Josh's Reality

Let me give you an example. Joshua is a thirty-five-year-old man married to Joan. Joan and Joshua have put a great deal of thought into financial planning. They bought an inexpensive house and paid it off in ten years. They've purchased used but well-maintained cars with cash. They have placed the maximum they can into retirement accounts.

But Josh's brother, Ken, lives from paycheck to paycheck. Ken, his wife, and his kids are overextended and maxed out financially. Ken drifts from job to job, blaming obnoxious bosses and impossible clients for his job-hopping. They spend first, pay later.

One day Ken calls his brother and asks for a $2,500 loan "just for a few months" because he knows Josh has a large savings account. Ken promises to pay it back, but Josh knows the real chances of that are slim. But, he ponders, what choice does he have? He and Joan have no kids or monthly payments. His brother is counting on him, and if he doesn't agree to loan Ken the money, his parents will call him "selfish" for "putting money over family." Although Joan and Josh are generous, their thrifty habits have already earned them the informal title of "Mr. and Mrs. Scrooge."

Joan's Reality

Josh's reality is that he had no choice. But his wife Joan, who comes from a family where personal limits were respected, doesn't see it that way at all. "Your brother *chose* to overspend and job-hop," she said. "Why should we reinforce his irresponsibility by bailing him out? Maybe it's a lesson he needs to learn and by giving him money we're not really doing him a favor."

"What am I supposed to do, watch my brother starve?" Joshua retorts.

"I don't think he'll starve," Joan says. "This is not a matter of life or death. This is a matter of giving up ballet lessons, a housekeeper, and cable TV."

In this scenario, Josh didn't want to earn his family's animosity. But since it was Joan's money, too, he had to say "no" to his brother. Just as he thought, Ken put up a fuss. But Joan's prediction also came true. Ken and his family were not forced onto the streets and did not subsist on peanut butter and jelly. Instead, Josh's parents bailed him out by getting a cash advance from their credit card (at 18 percent interest). And sure enough, Ken still hasn't paid it back. Still, Josh had to endure some discomfort when he "went against his family."

Lessons Learned

Although Joan was glad that they didn't get stuck with Ken's debts, she was unhappy that Josh had used her as the sole reason for the loan's decline. But she knew it was difficult for him to balance his needs with the needs of his family.

Josh and Joan told this story at a retreat for non-BPs, and several of us were trying to make Josh comprehend that as long as Ken knew he had a free ride, he wasn't going to change. We weren't getting through to Josh until out of frustration I whipped out my wallet and started handing dollar bills to him. "Do you want more?" I asked, filling his palm with cash. After a minute or two, confused, he said, "Stop."

Then another member of the group yelled, "I'll take the money!" and I turned and continued putting bills into someone else's palm until I was finally down to my credit cards. Finally Josh got the message: Ken would keep asking for money, going from crisis to crisis, as long as the money river flowed freely. More importantly, Josh finally caught on that since it was his money, he got to choose what to do with it.

"But what about the pressure from my family?" he asked.

"What about it?" I responded. "Are they going to call the police and report you for refusing to give someone a loan?"

He thought for a moment. "I'm forty years old. I don't need my family's approval."

"Bingo," I said.

Who Determines Your Reality?

Most non-BPs have been invalidated for so long that if you told them the sky was green, they'd believe it. A group of non-BPs from Welcome to Oz once got together in Wisconsin, where I live. Since I don't like cigarette smoke, I joked that by law, smoking was not permitted anywhere in the entire state of Wisconsin. I never imagined that anyone would take my comment seriously. But a smoker with a borderline mother and ex-husband nearly canceled her trip until I convinced her that no such law existed. Some restaurants and buildings banned smoking, yes. But how could they ban it everywhere in the entire state? She was relieved to know it was a joke.

So where is your reality coming from? From the BP in your life? From your parents? Your partner? If you're like most non-BPs, you have a difficult time listening to yourself and believing your own perceptions. It's one of the reasons you're using this workbook. Confidently forming your own opinion is one way of treasuring yourself. You have just as much right to do this as anyone else.

📖 Action Step 27:
Are You a Disappearing Person?

Author Beverly Engel (2000) shows how early influences set up some people to be what she calls "disappearing people." In a relationship, a "disappearing person" gives up part of himself in order for the relationship to continue. Engel's book is not about the relationship between BPs and non-BPs, but from my experience, some of its lessons are valuable for non-BPs. I have adapted this questionnaire from Engel's book to help you identify if you are a "disappearing person." Answer the following question with a "yes" or "no" based on your first, intuitive response.

1. Is there an implicit agreement that your BP's views are somehow "better" or more valid? ____

2. When a compromise needs to be made, are you usually the one making it? ____

3. Are you afraid to assert yourself because you're afraid you'll lose the other person's approval, friendliness, or the relationship itself? ____

4. Have you stopped doing things you used to enjoy to keep this relationship? ____

5. If your BP is your child, have you let your child's problems outweigh the rest of your family's needs? Your own needs? ____

6. If your BP is a new partner, did the relationship seem to come together very quickly and passionately? Do you spend most of your time daydreaming about this person? ____

7. If your BP is a longtime partner, have you forgotten what a "normal" relationship is like? ____

8. If your BP is a parent, do you still feel you need his or her approval even though you're past age eighteen? ____ If you answered "no," are you afraid of disclosing important parts of your life you know would meet with disapproval? ____

9. Do you question or devalue your own interpretation of events or opinions when they differ from your BP's? ____

10. Are you being dishonest by omitting crucial information or directly telling untruths in this relationship? ____

11. Do you wonder why you keep up this relationship even though it's almost all negative? ____

12. Do you feel what you bring to the relationship is valued and acknowledged? ____

13. Does this relationship keep you so occupied it doesn't leave much time for your own growth as a person? ____

14. Does this relationship keep you so occupied that you don't have time to work on your own problems because the BP's come first? ____

No matter who the BP in your life is, you have the right to be respected and treated with kindness. If the majority of your answers just now showed a lack of respect for you, your opinions, wants, and beliefs, you may be a disappearing person—especially if you are the adult child of a BP. But you can change this, and this chapter will show you how. The next step is identifying where you learned your role in the BP/non-BP "dance," to give you insight into why you are giving away pieces of yourself in this relationship. Again, I adapted the following questionnaire from Engel (2000).

📖 Action Step 28:
Why Do You Disappear?

Answer the following questions "yes" or "no." If the answer is "yes," rate the intensity of the problem from 1 to 3, with a 3 being the most intense. Base your answer on your *perception* of the problem. For example, if you grew up during World War II and your father went off to war, he may have left the family for a good reason. But as a child, you may not have been able to understand that and processed the information as "my father abandoned me."

* Do you feel that you had trouble bonding well with your parents? _____
  Rating _____

* Were one or both of your parents absent for a long time during your childhood—either away entirely through divorce or abandonment, through work or other preoccupations, or through alcoholism or substance abuse, or were they emotionally absent? _____
  Rating _____

* Were your needs neglected, either physically or emotionally? _____
  Rating _____

* Did your parents minimize, oppose, or make fun of your needs? _____
  Rating _____

* Were you physically or sexually abused by anyone, or forced to watch someone else being abused? This includes inappropriate touching, discussion, or sexual "joking" you could not control or understand. _____
  Rating _____

* Were you verbally or emotionally abused or repeatedly exposed to it? _____
  Rating _____

* Were you rejected or ridiculed by your parents, siblings, peers, or community? _____
  Rating _____

📖 *Action Step 34:*
DeFOGging Your Life

To deFOG your life, start by identifying places where you are vulnerable and installing FOG-alert devices. The following are examples to help you recognize the process.

Fear

"Anger seems to magnetize fear, pulling it quickly to the surface . . . for many of us, this emotion seems so dangerous that we're afraid of it in any form. And we fear not only other people's anger, but our own" (Forward and Frazier, 1997, 45).

On a scale of 1 to 5, with 1 being low and a 5 being high, how afraid are you of the following scenarios? Explain your fear in your notebook: Take your vague feeling and think as practically as possible. What exactly are you afraid of happening? What is your best- and worst-case scenario? Be as realistic as you can.

I am afraid of:

_____ Losing the BP's approval

_____ Getting the BP angry with me

_____ Getting the "silent treatment"

_____ The BP getting into danger

_____ The BP getting into legal trouble

_____ BP attempting suicide

_____ BP self-harming

_____ BP getting depressed

_____ Being thought of as "selfish"

_____ Change

_____ Taking responsibility

_____ Being found out

_____ Being a bad partner

_____ Being a bad son/daughter/parent

_____ Being a bad friend

_____ Fear of abandonment

_____ Fear of retaliation

_____ People thinking that I'm a bad person

_____ Trying something new

_____ Losing the relationship

_____ Loss of love/friendship/companionship

_____ Losing contact with or custody of my children

_____ Distortion campaigns

_____ Being alone

_____ Living by myself

_____ Taking care of certain practical matters

_____ Being called names

_____ Being embarrassed in public

_____ Being threatened

_____ Being falsely arrested

_____ Hitting someone

_____ Becoming depressed

_____ Failing to live up to expectations

_____ Confrontation

_____ Getting angry

_____ Losing control

Obligation

"When our sense of obligation is stronger than our sense of self-respect and self-caring, blackmailers quickly learn how to take advantage" (Forward and Frazier, 1997, 51).

On a scale of 1 to 5, how obligated do you feel about the following things? Again, explain your answers in your notebook: Why do you feel obligated? Where is it written that you are obligated? Who obligated you? What do you feel obligated to do? Be as realistic and as reasonable as possible.

_____ I think of myself as a good partner/friend/child/parent.

_____ The BP needs me.

_____ The BP gave me something(s) and I should be grateful.

_____ People are supposed to love their partner/friend/child/parent.

_____ I am trying to live up to the expectations of my partner/friend/child/parent.

_____ Since BPD is a brain disorder I am obligated to make adjustments.

_____ If I didn't do this, people would think badly of me.

____ I put this much time into this relationship; why quit now?

____ People like me have a duty.

____ My religion teaches me to be this way.

____ My parents taught me that I should do this.

____ If I didn't live up to my obligations, I would feel like a bad person.

____ My values prevent me.

____ The BP never fails to remind me.

Guilt

"Emotional blackmailers encourage us to take global responsibility for their complaints and unhappiness, doing all they can to reprogram the basic and necessary mechanisms of appropriate guilt into an undeserved guilt-production line where the lights continually flash 'guilty, guilty, guilty'" (Forward and Frazier, 1997, 54).

Fill in the blanks in the lines below to make the statements specific to your life. Then, on a scale of 1 to 5, rate your sense of guilt. Again, write in your notebook: Why do you feel guilty? Where is it written that you are guilty? Who served as judge and jury? How long is your sentence? Be as realistic and as reasonable as possible.

____ I feel guilty for feeling _____ instead of _____ .

____ I hate confrontation so much that I just say "I'm sorry" and hope that ends it.

____ I feel like a bad person when _____ .

____ If I had known about BPD earlier, I wouldn't have messed everything up.

____ When the BP feels _____ she blames it on me.

____ I would _____ if it weren't for the fact that I would feel guilty.

____ The BP blames me for a lot of things.

____ Sometimes I feel guilty for thinking _____ .

____ Sometimes I feel guilty for doing _____ .

____ Sometimes I feel guilty for being _____ .

____ Sometimes I feel guilty for having _____ .

____ I did something years ago that I still feel guilty about.

____ My _____ told me I was guilty for _____ .

____ Sometimes I feel guilty for wishing the BP was dead.

Cutting through the FOG

In real life, fog can lead to collisions, people getting lost, and general confusion. FOG can do the same thing. FOG destroys relationships because the people who exploit it and those who let themselves be exploited are not acting out of love or caring. Real love isn't won by manipulation. It only leads to anger, burnout, resentment, and sometimes the loss of the relationship. When you eliminate the FOG, BPs can clearly ask for what they want and non-BPs can choose to give it because that is what they genuinely want to do.

📖 Action Step 35:
Techniques to Combat FOG

Violinists do not wake up one day and decide to play a concerto with the New York Philharmonic. For every minute you see in performance, they may have practiced for six months. Some smokers quit several times before they quit for good. Even if you've tried to combat emotional blackmail before and been less than successful, you can still do it once you've learned and practiced the techniques.

In the following exercise, you can practice combating emotional blackmail. Like many other life changes, it's a skill that requires *inner motivation*, a *commitment to change*, *practice*, and *follow-through*.

Inner Motivation: Calculate the costs of giving in to emotional blackmail. Check off those costs that are appropriate to your situation.

_____ Feelings of anger, irritation, being used, being trapped, stressed, burned out, manipulated, confused, resentful, hurt, frustrated, overwhelmed, unlovable, discouraged.

_____ Loss of self-respect, control, integrity; loss of time for yourself, of time you had planned for yourself or others; loss of pleasure in the relationship; loss of possibilities to be a good role model for others.

_____ Other problems: feeling forced to agree when you disagree; being thought of as a "softy"; feeling discouraged when you try to stand up for yourself; being more concerned about what others think of you than what you think of yourself; avoiding places where you might run into the blackmailer; and not feeling in charge of your own life. Worst of all (at least in an adult relationship you've chosen) is that you are not happy with a situation *you agreed to of your own accord.*

Commitment to Change: Make a "commitment to change" certificate in your notebook. Write out a contract with yourself, spelling out your personal limits. What do you want to do? Under what conditions are you willing to accommodate others? How often? Will you expect anything in return? You must make the benefits tangible so it feels like you are gaining something: reclaiming your integrity. Don't worry if you're not perfect. No one is—especially people learning a new skill.

Practice: If you have a hard time saying "no" to anyone, start with declining simple requests you don't want to do for people who do not have BPD. Just like our violinist did not start with the New York Philharmonic, don't start with the BP in your life. Look for other opportunities when less is at stake and the people making the request do not have a personality disorder. Take an assertiveness class. Learn to walk before you learn to run.

Forward (1997) recommends that you *do not defend or explain your decision to the blackmailer.* This may seem like a bold step—you may think, "At least I offer him an explanation." But most of the time you actually don't. Now, if you and your partner agreed to have children and you changed your mind, the situation would be different. But if you try to explain every decision you make and feel the need to justify and explain it, you may be talking apples while your BP is talking oranges. The point is you want to change your way of life while someone else is seeing a particular request in isolation. Excuses only give the BP ammunition.

Let's say that the BP assumes you will be there to pick her up after outpatient surgery. A very understandable request. But let's say that she rarely asks or understands that you have to take off work or otherwise rearrange your schedule and you feel taken for granted. The more you try to explain, the more the BP will push your "obligation" and "guilt" buttons. If you simply but firmly say, "It's just not going to work out for me this time," instead of "I have to work," you don't give her anything to work with, such as, "What's more important, me or your job?"

Follow-through: Repeat the following phrases as often as necessary and do not fall into the trap of explaining your decision. Some people only listen to explanations to find a flaw in reasoning so that they can back you into a corner. Think of a small child asking, "Why can't I eat all my Halloween candy now?" a dozen times while you tick off twelve reasons.

* I'm sorry, I won't be able to.

* I'm sorry that makes you upset.

* I just can't do that.

* I understand you feel that way, but I'm going to have to say no.

* That's your choice. This is mine.

* I understand I've done that before, but this time I can't.

* Let's talk about this when you're less upset.

* You may have a point, but I can't do it this time.

* I understand you feel that way. I hope you find another solution.

* I see you're disappointed. I hope you find another answer to your problem.

* Threatening me isn't going to work. I've made my decision and I'm asking you to respect that.

* Come up with your own phrase to use as a response to emotional blackmail

---

📖 Action Step 36: Anticipate and Practice

In your notebook, anticipate an entire conversation in which you are being emotionally blackmailed. What is the blackmailer likely to want? What pressure or threats will he use? Go back to your worst case/best case scenario. Remember that each person is responsible for his own actions. That means you own your decision and the blackmailer owns his. Changes are highly likely that you will feel uncomfortable with it at first. But chances are good that no one will turn into a frog, go to hell, or end up begging on the street. Each time you do this successfully, you will gain a newfound respect for yourself and become more confident. And it will be easier to do the next time.

If the BP notices a change in your outlook and says so, avoid saying something that could imply "I'm putting myself first, now." While that may be true, saying it would push a very hot fear-of-abandonment button. Simply say, "I feel I am doing what is best for both of us. I'm sorry if you don't agree." Because you *are* doing it for both of you. The better you can meet your own needs in this relationship, the more likely it is that the relationship will improve.

Keep the Benefits in Mind

Change will be difficult for both you and the blackmailer. So it's vital to keep in mind that you're doing this both to reclaim your life and to ensure the health of the relationship. You won't be happy in the long term in a relationship in which you feel you're being blackmailed. Most likely, ending the relationship or detaching yourself emotionally would be much, much more painful than coping with blackmail. At the same time, you're teaching the BP healthier ways to get what he needs while you take care of you. Keep telling yourself, "I *can* stand this feeling. This is what it feels like to make adult choices. This is normal."

Now that we've discussed the basics of emotional blackmail, we'll take an overall look at choosing the right words and knowing which path to take when trying to be heard by someone who has Borderline Personality Disorder.

Chapter 9

Being Heard: Communicating with a Borderline

It's scary, telling another person "This is who I am. This is what I want."
Scarier still is standing by the truth about ourselves—our integrity—as we
must when we give the other person a choice to accept or not accept our
decisions and differences ... But remembter we're asking for something that
is absolutely reasonable: We want the other person to stop manipulating us.

—Susan Forward, *Emotional Blackmail*

Choosing the Right Communications Method

Since writing *Stop Walking on Eggshells* (Mason and Kreger 1998), I have spoken with dozens of non-BPs about being heard when communicating with a BP, whether it be reacting to rages, responding to low-functioning BPs, enduring snippy remarks and sarcasm, or having your point of view acknowledged. I've learned that the number one problem is that each of these situations calls for a different communication method, and most non-BPs don't realize this.

It can seem overwhelming and a lot to learn. But using the wrong method is like trying to eat soup with a fork. You need to learn different methods for different situations and practice them so that they become second nature to you. It may be like learning a foreign language, but if you're going to have a relationship with this person, there is no way to avoid communicating. Even silence communicates. In this chapter, I will address different situations that call for different communication methods.

Listening Abilities and Capabilities

Biological studies seem to show that people with BPD and others who undergo "trauma" (however the subject defines it) at an early age may be hardwired differently. When emotions are very high, they can't "hear" you, no matter what you're saying.

Here's what's happening: the emotional part of the brain is taking over in the same way that shock and denial help protect people who have just suffered a loss. Intellectually, they understand what's happening. But the "emotional" part of the brain is crowding out the cognitive (thinking) part. Imagine a clogged sink. The water (rational thinking) is mostly blocked by built-up hair, scum, and whatever else is in there from the past (the emotions).

This is one reason why being intelligent is a handicap for both the BP and the non-BP. The non-BP keeps expecting things to make sense. How can they be at fault for something that happened *before they met the BP*? How can they "win" when they're damned if they do and damned if they don't? The more time non-BPs spend searching for logical answers, the longer they will elude them. And the smarter the non-BP is, the more difficult it is to understand why the BP behaves in ways that are counterproductive to what the BP wants.

Using DEAR with Ragers

If the BP is a rager, choose a time of relative calm to set a limit regarding rages. Use DEAR methods (see chapter 7) at a time when the BP is able to listen and respond. Tell the BP that you will not endure rages and you will only talk to the BP when he is able to have a meaningful conversation. Explain that if he gets angry, you will simply leave the room or otherwise exit until he can have a reasonable, two-way conversation.

If during this discussion the BP goes into a rage, leave the room and try to set the limit at another time. If the BP simply won't listen, leave, just as you would if someone were holding a knife and threatening to use it. Would you ask for the person's permission to get out of the way? Verbal abuse can be just as dangerous, though people tend to take it less seriously. Do not expose yourself or your children to cutting verbal remarks. If you disagree and want to argue during a borderline rage, at least get the children to safety, just as you would if they were being physically threatened. Verbal abuse is more insidious and just as dangerous to their mental health.

If your BP rages when you are out together and you are unable or unwilling to leave, do not get into the car with the BP. Take another car if you have to. Take the bus. Skip the trip. Buy a unicycle. Get a ride. *Do not put yourself in the position of being trapped with the BP.* Be creative. There was a time when we had no cars.

After you set the limit, you must follow through with it. If the BP rages, calmly remind him of your limit and leave (or whatever else you planned as a countermove). *Make sure to tell him when you will be back so that his abandonment fears are addressed.* This is very important. If the BP cannot control himself around the children, take them somewhere else. Do not allow children to be raged at or even to witness rages. If the BP is your minor child and you can't leave, protect yourself and any siblings. Tell the child you won't talk to him while he's screaming obscenities at you. If necessary, lock yourself in your bedroom with the other children. If you think the BP might hurt the pets, gather up the animals as well. If you still feel unsafe or worry that the BP child might harm himself, call 911.

📖 *Action Step 37: Leaving during a Rage*

The following are several ways to "leave." Check the ones that you can use.

_____ Hang up the phone.

_____ Go to a different room.

_____ Take the laundry and go to a laundromat.

_____ Delete e-mail. Filter out the BP's mail.

_____ Take a taxi.

_____ Put on the stereo headphones.

_____ Take the kids to a place of their choosing.

_____ Visit a friend.

_____ Arrange ahead of time for a friend to pick you up. Call him and wait outside at a previously designated place out of sight of the BP.

____ If you are afraid for your physical safety, have a bag packed ahead of time with necessary items and plan where you will go. Call 911 if you need to. Always document and file a report with the police.

Think of your own method and describe it in the blank space below.

_____

_____

_____

The Keys to Being Heard with Low-Functioning BPs

Low-functioning BPs may interpret innocent comments in ways the speaker doesn't intend, and may even think their loved one is putting them down. Therefore, when a lower-functioning BP is in the "BPD zone"—when BP behavior is triggered in a normally lucid person—you need to be careful about what you say.

Teresa Whitehurst, Ph.D., teaches families of BPs how to recognize BPD symptoms, predict triggers, and use verbal, nonverbal and other forms of communication in an attempt to offer empathy and avoid triggering symptoms. She teaches them how to word their sentences carefully to help diffuse potentially explosive situations. Her experience tends to be with families of lower-functioning BPs since it is these BPs who tend to use mental health services (higher-functioning BPs don't think they need them).

"To people who are diagnosed with BPD, words make a huge difference in how they feel about themselves, others, and the future," Whitehurst told me in an interview. "Family members who learn to accurately translate the BP's 'language' more than 50 percent of the time heighten their sense of safety, of being okay, and of being heard and understood."

Whitehurst recommends that family members watch for small signs and subtle mood shifts that can warn non-BPs of pending rages or acting out *before* they happen. "Translation is only the first step of the process, however," she says. "You need the right words to respond to mood shifts, angry accusations, or acting-out behaviors with empathy instead of anger."

Whitehurst has found that certain phrases more than others help BPs feel that their family members are sensitive to their feelings and needs. In my experience, most non-BPs feel that things should be the other way around—that BPs should be more sensitive to *them*. This may be true. But BPD can prevent people from validating you just like a damaged spinal cord can prevent people from walking. If you look at the situation this way—that you are helping the BP do something they don't have the tools to do—you can feel better about the extra effort it takes to learn these communication skills.

Whitehurst says, "Attuning ourselves to people with BPD with accurate translation and empathetic responses serves to encourage them to use the highest level of communication—verbal communication—and can calm the agitated (and sometimes crisis-provoking) emotions and fears common to BPD."

Practice, Practice, Practice

Whitehurst recommends practicing certain phrases with friends and other family members before you attempt to use them in a heated situation with your BP. These phrases appear in the following exercise.

📖 Action Step 38:
Memorize These Phrases

Using index cards, write down the following phrases, filling in the blanks with a variety of responses. Carry them with you, and memorize them while you are standing in line, waiting, or have a free minute or two.

1. "To me, it sounds like you may be feeling a little _____ ."

2. "I'm hearing _____ . Are you feeling _____ because of _____ ?"

3. "I'm wondering if something I've said or done might have contributed to your feeling irritable/angry/anxious _____ ."

4. "I may be wrong about this, but I'm wondering if you're feeling kind of lonely/let down/betrayed/discouraged _____ ?"

5. "If this had happened to me, I would be feeling _____ . How about you?"

6. "I feel _____ when you begin _____ ."

7. Can we continue this discussion in about _____ (minutes/hours)?"

Using "I" Statements

All of the sentences in the preceding exercise have two things in common:

1. They begin with the word "I." You're the world's leading expert on your own feelings. No one can take them away, dub them "justified" or "unjustified," or change them, although you can change them yourself. If the BP does say, "You shouldn't feel that way," simply say, "But I do. Feelings don't always make sense and they don't have to. Feelings just are. I respect yours and I hope you can respect mine."

2. The statements don't presume to know how the BP feels. Even if the BP is raging louder than a car alarm at 1 A.M., she may deny or be unaware of her anger. She may be sobbing like Niagara Falls, yet deny that she's sad. And perhaps they're tears of joy. Being concerned without assuming what's on the BP's mind or at her emotional center can lead to better communication.

"By using responses such as these more or less consistently over time, you can eventually transform your BP's relationship with you," Whitehurst explains. "If the person with BPD is in therapy, this modification can provide a powerful boost to your BP's efforts to grow in emotional self-control, maturity, and self-esteem."

What to Remember

_____ Remember that phrases, however brilliantly they're used, can't cure BPD. Additionally, phrases may work some of the time but not all of the time. This doesn't mean you've failed. It simply means that every situation is different.

_____ Don't chastise yourself for forgetting these phrases, and accept that this new language will not be appropriate every time. No change works overnight, and you've been communicating in other ways for months or years. Just like there's no diet pill that keeps the fat off painlessly and permanently, communication techniques are not cures but *tools* that can help when used correctly in the right circumstances with the right person in the best frame of mind.

_____ When your BP suddenly becomes depressed, angry, or argumentative, it's easy to fall into old, quarrelsome patterns. Writing down or, better yet, memorizing a variety of responses for different situations can get both of you onto a more positive path, when you find yourself faced with an unexpected quarrel or emotional state:

Different Responses for Different Moods

People with BPD—children especially—can easily change the mood of an entire household within thirty seconds. By changing your responses from combative to collaborative, you may be able to avert an argument or temper tantrum.

The following are some of Whitehurst's suggested responses for different moods. This table expands on the previous list of responses and indicates appropriate versus inappropriate responses to different situations.

Situation	Weak Responses	Wise Responses
BP's mood seems to be sinking, *although he hasn't said so.*	Cheer up. Do you want to see a movie? What's the problem?	I may be wrong, but you seem a little down. How are you feeling? It might help to talk about how you're feeling. When would you like to talk? I'm wondering what would help you right now?
BP *tells you* that he is feeling anxious, sad, irritable, and depressed.	What is it *now*? Don't be sad. Don't take it out on me. Don't worry.	Do you want to talk about it? Is there some way I can help? It's great you're telling me how you feel in words; this helps me understand you better.
BP is *showing you his feelings by acting-in or out;* crying, screaming, slamming doors, throwing things, cursing, the silent treatment.	Stop it, leave me alone. Control yourself, act like an adult. Are you mad at me? You're acting spoiled. Please talk to me. I'm so worried about you. As long as you're living under my roof, you'll do what I say! Get out of my face.	I can see how upset you are and I'd like to talk with you about the situation if you calm down a bit. I love you and I want to hear what's going on in your mind and heart. But I can't help you until you can sit down and talk to me. What would help you calm down right now? I can't hear your complaints against me until I feel safe. If you're feeling extremely angry or out of control, let's take a break and then meet to talk about it later. I promise to listen.

Responding to Incorrect Assumptions

BPs are often so caught up in their own emotions they make false assumptions about what you do and say. If the BP doesn't understand your reasoning, try one or more of the following sample responses from Whitehurst.

* "If I've said or done anything to cause you distress, I hope you'll tell me."

* "Sounds like when I said that, you started to feel sad/anxious/stressed/annoyed/distracted."

* "No wonder you're feeling angry/worried/disappointed/confused."

* "I hope you'll believe me when I say I didn't *intend* any harm when I said/did that, yet it sounds like my statement/action nonetheless did cause you distress/difficulty."

* "I hope that you can forgive me. I also hope you hear me when I say that I didn't *intend* this result/problem/feeling for you."

* "I'm wondering if we can think of ways to prevent this kind of problem in the future: do you have some ideas?"

Snippy Remarks and Sarcasm

Snippy or sarcastic comments are difficult to respond to because they're often vague, indirect, and meant to hurt (not to communicate). It's the verbal equivalent of a schoolyard bully taunting someone to "push me," to give him an excuse to smack you in the face. So the best way to handle these kinds of statements is to minimize them, purposely misunderstand their intent, and avoid giving them the importance that the BP would like them to have.

Responding to Sarcasm

Don't defend yourself, explain, justify, counterattack—all of which just embroil you in an argument—or just withdraw, which implies you will let yourself be verbally abused. Instead, do one or more of the following:

* Pretend ignorance of malicious intent. If the BP says, "Boy, that chocolate cake sure has a lot of calories," implying you shouldn't eat it, you might say, "I know, isn't it great?"

* Recognize that your critic has an opinion, even if you don't agree. If the BP says, "I can't believe you'd do that!" you might say, "No you wouldn't." If your BP teen says, "I can't believe you won't let me go to Aaron's party, just because his parents are away. I hate you!" you might say, "I know it seems to you as if we're the meanest parents on the planet, but that's the way it is."

* If your BP says something sarcastic or makes negative comments about an opinion you've expressed, make a noncommittal, vague comment, such as, "Some people think that way," or "Whatever you say." Say it in a carefree way that shows you don't particularly care about his opinion. Rephrasing someone else's inane or careless remark as a question often just shows how illogical it is. If your BP says, "You can't go to the park because it's 2 P.M. and we eat dinner at 6 P.M." respond with, "So you're saying we can't go to the park now at 2 P.M. because we're eating dinner at 6 P.M.?"

Here are the two most important points to remember:

1. Don't let a hurtful comment go unacknowledged, even if your response is to get up and walk away, saying you have important things to do. Over time, little drops of venom build up and become very toxic to your mental health.

2. Don't show you take the comments seriously by arguing or doing what the BP is doing.

📖 Action Step 39:
Practice, Practice, and Practice Some More

New ways of reacting do not come automatically. You need to work on change for it to be effective.

1. Think back and write the BP's typical sarcastic comments in your notebook.

2. Using possible responses given in this chapter as a guideline, write down the answers that feel most comfortable for you.

3. When you are alone, practice saying each of these phrases out loud. Keep saying them until you feel the words rolling smoothly off your tongue.

4. Write down an imagined response by the BP.

5. Practice repeating the same phrase (the "broken record" technique). Envision yourself remaining calm and in control. Take deep breaths and visualize yourself repeating the comments until you can do so without your heart beating faster or until your sense of discomfort fades. No matter what the BP says, simply repeat your response. Pretend the BP is dangling a fishhook at you, daring you to bite and drag you into an argument. You simply have to refuse to take the bait.

6. Go to a good friend, explain what you are doing, and ask the friend to play the part of the BP. If she doesn't know what the BP would say, show her the responses you anticipate in the notebook. Practice this until you feel comfortable. Make sure you feel comfortable with all possible BP responses, from raging to the silent treatment. If you don't know someone you can ask to play the BP's role, use a tape recorder to record the comments you imagine the BP will make. Then you can practice responding, using the tape you've made.

Having Your Point of View Acknowledged

At some point, many BPs are able to have an actual discussion without raging or being biting. At these times, they are the most open to your point of view. But it's a two-way street, and you will probably have to show good faith first by showing that you are listening to what they are saying. This kind of conversation takes the most skill.

The following is a simple three-step technique you can use during the entire conversation. It requires *repeating* what the BP said, *responding* to it with feeling and using "I" statements, and *acknowledging* you may have two different opinions.

Step 1: Repeating.

Repeat (quote or paraphrase) the BP's point while making eye contact. This does not mean you are agreeing with her. You are simply showing that you have heard her. *When people feel heard, they feel better, even if the other person hasn't agreed with them.*

You need to work on listening to the BP, rather than waiting for your turn to talk. Simply listen and understand the point(s) well enough to repeat them. If you need to, ask the BP to slow down. After you have repeated what the BP said, ask "Is this what you meant to say?" If not, ask her to repeat it.

At first, simply repeat what the BP says. After you feel comfortable with this, try to include a "feeling phrase," asking the BP if she is feeling a certain way.

📖 Action Step 40:
Repeating Phrases

When you repeat what the BP has said, it is important that you don't sound condescending, angry, or patronizing. You don't want to sound like you're simply parroting phrases. Try to achieve a tone that says, "I'm listening closely to what you're saying." Fill in the following helpful phrases using words that paraphrase comments your BP has made. Write them down in your notebook.

* So what you're saying is you believe that . . . ?

* You seem to think that . . . Is this right?

* So, if I have this right, you want . . . ?

* Let me make sure I am hearing you. You want me to . . . ?

* You say you believe that . . . Is that what you meant to say?

* It's sounds like you're feeling . . . Am I right?

Now, practice these phrases until you memorize them and can say them aloud with the right tone of voice. Practice by saying them to a friend who is willing to play the role of the BP.

Step 2: Responding

In a perfect world, you would respond to your BP's comments and the BP would confirm that he understands you by repeating what *you* said. But this is probably not possible in Oz because it requires skills the BP may not have. However, you can validate yourself simply by making your own statement and reassuring yourself that you, like the BP, have a right to your point of view, opinions, and reactions. I strongly recommend that even if you have a therapist, you surround yourself with a group of friends who will listen to you vent. If you are lucky, one of them will be especially witty and will have you laughing instead of crying in sadness or frustration.

Many years ago, I was faced with a serious situation involving a child of someone with BPD. I used to get together with a friend who was equally angry, and we would make up songs about the BP that he would never hear. Even though I knew all about the BP's pain and why he did what he did, it didn't make me feel any better. So she and I would make up songs about him, using familiar melodies and changing the words. We would take turns, competing to see who could come up with the most outrageous lyrics. During a three-hour car trip, we must have exhausted every tune I know. Today, I remember the fun of singing those songs more than I remember the frustration over the entire situation. And since no one heard the songs but us, no one was hurt.

An "I" statement is one that cannot be argued with. If a child says, "My little brother acts like a monster," you can respond with your own opinion of the little brother's behavior. But if the child says, "I am jealous of my little brother," you cannot tell her she doesn't feel that way. She does feel that way. You can try to help her feel less jealous by spending more time with her, but you cannot (or should not) tell her what to feel. *Feelings are not right or wrong, justified or unjustified. They just are.* Make sure your feeling statement is *not* an opinion, such as "I feel you are wrong." A feeling is some variation on mad, sad, glad, scared, or confused. You can follow up the feeling statement with another "I" statement that describes your opinion or point of view.

Rather than argue with the BP's reality, simply put yours next to his. For example, if your BP said, "I hate bees," you would *not* say, "You should like bees because they play an important role in pollination." You might say, "I appreciate bees. Without them, plants might not get pollinated." It may be a subtle difference, but you don't need to contradict or invalidate the BP's views or feelings to present your own.

Feeling and "I" Statements

What follows are some examples of feelings and "I" statements. You can fill in the blanks with words appropriate to your own circumstance.

* "I don't feel that way. I feel ..."

* "I feel misunderstood. My intention was to ..."

* "I am confused about that statement. What do you mean?"

* "I feel differently about that. My opinion is ..."

* "I am sorry you believe that I meant to hurt you. When I said ... my intention was to ..."

* "I love ... and would never purposely do anything to ..."

📖 *Action Step 41:*
Choose the Right Response

Read the following pairs of responses. Circle the one that is a feeling and "I" statement, the response that is less likely to start an argument. The correct answers are at the end of the chapter.

1. a) "You never heard me say that I hated you."

   b) "I don't hate you, I love you."

2. a) "I enjoy my work and I think my commitment to it will be rewarded."

   b) "You're wrong. I am not spending too much time at work, and if I spend too much time there, maybe it's because I don't want to come home."

3. a) "I like having the privacy of my own house, and I appreciate being called in advance if you want to come over."

   b) "It is rude to come over without calling me. Don't do it anymore."

4. a) "I refuse to let you treat your sister that way. It's rude and thoughtless."

   b) "As Sara's mother, I feel responsible for making sure she is safe and not afraid of how she will be treated."

Step 3: Acknowledging

Rather than argue your position, simply acknowledge that you both have the right to your own feelings and opinions about whatever the subject is. Sample phrases include:

* I guess we can agree to disagree.

* Let's say we both have our own opinions and leave it at that.

* I understand. You feel that . . . and I believe that . . . There are always at least two ways to look at something.

Advanced Communication Techniques

When you feel confident using the previous communication model, you may want to try one that is a bit more complex. I call it PUVAS. This technique can be used to respond to a borderline who is projecting, accusing, being overly blaming or critical, or who is making unreasonable demands. PUVAS stands for:

* **Pay attention.**

* Understand fully.

* Validate the BP's emotions.

* Assert yourself with your own reality statement.

* Shift responsibility for the BPs feelings and actions back to the BP or share the responsibility with the BP.

To simplify this technique, look at it in two steps: the PUV, which is for the BP, and the AS, which addresses your needs. *The steps must be done in the right order, and none of them should be skipped.* As with the previous technique, PUVAS cannot be attempted if the BP is snipping, being sarcastic, raging, or being abusive. Those call for other techniques covered earlier in this chapter. Following is a description of how to use PUVAS.

Pay attention. When it is your turn to listen, really listen. Don't think about what you are going to say. Do not become defensive and tune out the borderline, even if she is accusing you of things you never did or said. You will have the chance to address this later. This will accomplish two things: it will help you validate the BP's feelings and it will assist you in detecting emotions that may lie beneath the surface.

Understand fully. Make sure you gently challenge any vague generalizations you don't understand. Ask the BP to elaborate. Ask him to be specific without sounding like you are grilling him. Your goal is to find out exactly what is causing problems for him and to help him see that words like "always" or "never" may be misperceptions. Again, don't defend yourself.

Validate the BP's emotions. The BP's feelings may not make sense to you, but they do to the BP. Find the nugget of gold in the cup of sand and respond affirmatively to this, even if all you can say is "I understand that you feel . . ." and repeat the feeling that the BP has expressed. Do not judge the feelings, deny them, trivialize them, or discuss whether you think they are "justified." Ask the BP if your perceptions are correct (she will *not* want to be told how she feels, even if you think it is obvious), and show the BP that you are hearing her emotions. Avoid sounding patronizing or condescending; the BP may get enraged if you do not sound like you are taking her concerns seriously.

Assert yourself with your own reality statements. Some reality statements will be factual, such as, "When I said that I smelled something burning, I wasn't commenting on your cooking. I was just noticing a burning odor." Some reality statements will reflect your opinions: "I don't believe that wanting to see a movie with friends is selfish. I think that even when two people are married, it's good for them both to have other friends and pursue their own interests." Naturally, the BP will most likely have a different opinion on what you meant or the place of friends in a marriage. Don't debate. Just reiterate what you believe and accept that the two of you will disagree on this matter. You don't have to agree on everything.

You may decide to negotiate—go out with your friends on certain days and not others. Or you may be firm and unwilling to compromise. Don't explain or leave openings for the BP to argue with you. Say, "This is what I need. I understand you or someone else might feel differently, but we're not all the same, and this is what *I* need in this relationship."

Shift responsibility for the BP's feelings and actions back to the BP. You can let him know that you can support him, but he is ultimately the only person who can make himself feel better.

The following conversation is an example of PUVAS being used by Richard, a non-BP, who is having a discussion with his girlfriend Sara. No matter how angry or upset Sara gets, Richard remains calm and composed.

Sara: I know you made a pass at my best friend, Barbara.

Richard: What makes you think that?

Sara: I saw you talking together, I saw the way you were looking at her, and you were off together away from the rest of us at the party. You can't fool me.

Richard: Whoa, let's take this one at a time. Why do you doubt my love for you?

Sara: You don't think I'm sexy enough for you, for one thing.

Richard: You said I don't think you're sexy. Can you tell me what I've done that gave you that idea?

Sara: We usually have sex on the weekend, and this weekend you didn't make one move in my direction.

In this situation, asking Sara to elaborate gave Richard some much needed information. If he had immediately responded by denying the accusation, they probably would have fought at length without uncovering the real issue: Sara's fear of abandonment sparked by a change in their sexual routine. The conversation continued.

Richard: You sound really upset and angry. I can see that from the tone of your voice and the expression on your face. Sara, I can understand that if you thought I didn't find you sexually attractive, that would be upsetting. Are you feeling hurt and sad right now?

Sara: Yes!

Richard then offered his "reality statement," asserting his point of view.

Richard: We spent the weekend remodeling the bathroom and I thought we were both tired and out of sorts. I do find you very sexy. But I was tired and I thought you were feeling tired and grubby, too.

Richard's last step was to shift responsibility for the BP's feelings back to the BP herself. He lets Sara know that he can support her, but she is ultimately the only person who can make herself feel better.

Richard: It sounds to me like you think I have sexually abandoned or rejected you completely just because of one weekend. But think of all the other great sex we've had at other times. I'm not sure why one sex-less weekend would convince you I'm attracted to someone else, but I do know I don't feel that way and I didn't knowingly do anything to cause you to think that.

Even the best communication method doesn't get rid of the personality disorder. At some point, you will need to make decisions about the relationship and your investment in it, which is what I will cover in the next chapter.

Answers to Action Step 41:
1. B
2. A
3. A
4. B

Part 2

Making Wise Decisions and Implementing Them

Chapter 10

Considering Options and Making Decisions

I feel like a cartoon character in mid-flight across the canyon, wondering if I'm going to fall in or bridge the gap to the other side....

—Judith Viorst, *Necessary Losses*

Your options are very different, depending upon the type of relationship you are in. So I will take each relationship separately. No matter what type of relationship you're in, you can use Action Step 16 from chapter 5 to help remind you of what you really want out of life.

What to Do If the BP Is Your Partner

Some non-BPs take months. Some take years. But eventually they all come to some sort of decision about what they can do to make their life more livable if their partner refuses to change.

Naturally, their first considerations are usually practical: the children (if there are any), money, etc. But let's put these issues aside for a moment because we want to get at *what you really want*. You may decide to set your interests aside for various reasons later, but it's essential to know where you stand and what you want out of life. After all, you can't get it unless you know what it is. And once you're committed to what you want, you'll be more willing to work to make these changes happen.

Mira Kirshenbaum (1996) believes that when most people who are ambivalent try to make a decision about a relationship, they make a list of "pros" on one side of a piece of paper and a list of "cons" on the other side.

But that approach, she says, is too similar to acting like an attorney (digging up evidence) and a jury (making the decision). Different considerations are not of equal weight, and relationships do not stay static. Plus, need I remind you that of all partners, one with BPD is most likely to refuse to be pinned down?

Instead, Kirshenbaum believes in diagnosing your relationship the way a doctor would: searching for clues that separately or together will make your course of action clear. While her advice applies to relationships in general, it is useful to think about in terms of BPD. I've modified some of her questions and commentary to specifically address BPD relationships. Write the answers and your thoughts in your notebook.

📖 *Action Step 42:*
Diagnosing the Relationship

Answer the following questions in your notebook.

* When you think about the times when things were best, had you settled into a period of real intimacy and knowledge about your partner? Or were you still in the putting-on-your-best-face early stages of the relationship? In other words, are you longing for the person your BP actually was, or the person she was pretending to be?

* Look at your index cards from Action Step 16. Review the cards that list high priorities that the BP cannot or will not fulfill. How important are the

needs that he cannot fulfill, and how long are you willing to wait to see if he will try to fulfill your other needs?

* Has there been more than one instance of physical violence toward you or any children? If so, I advise you to seriously consider leaving, and if you haven't done so, make sure you put together a safety plan (appendix C).

* Take a coin from your pocket. Flip it. Heads, you stay, tails, you leave. Watch the coin fall. Now stop and close your eyes. Before you open them, pretend it's heads. How do you feel? Pretend it's tails. How do you feel? When the coin lands, you may find your true feelings emerging.

* Does your partner seem to deliberately avoid giving you what you need—even the smallest little thing? If so, she may have an above average need for power and control. This gets old very fast and is an intimacy destroyer.

* Has this progressed to the point where you feel invisible or humiliated most of the time? Does he shut you up when you want to talk about things that are important to you? Is your self-esteem so tiny you couldn't find it even with a police sniffing dog? You don't need a counselor to tell you this relationship is toxic to your self-esteem.

* Is your partner a habitual liar? Would they rather lie than tell the truth? Is this such a problem you've become cynical?

* When you think about all that you've given in this relationship, do you suppose it's realistic to expect the score will ever be evened up? If not, does this bother you?

* Does your partner take any responsibility for the problems in the relationship? Has she told you this won't change? After five years of studying BPD, I have found that willingness to look at problems *together* is a better predictor of long-term success than any other factor.

* Have you fallen into the "waiting trap"? The trap works like this: say you push the button for the up elevator. You wait. One minute. Two. Three. Soon you realize that you only need to go up two flights and the stairs are right there. But now it's been four minutes. You're sure the elevator will come about the same time you open the door to the stairs. Besides, you've already waited five—no, six minutes. At seven minutes, the elevator arrives. It takes another three minutes to load and unload everyone. Congratulations. You've fallen into the waiting trap. A five-minute trip has taken ten. The marriage waiting trap works much like this. If you've been waiting five years for your partner to change, what's another year or two or three? But three years becomes thirty and nothing has changed.

* Give yourself a reasonable date for the BP to make changes you've requested. If she hasn't made them by then, there's a good chance she never will.

* Remember that actions speak louder than words.

* Are you limiting even the good times with your partner for fear they will turn into bad times: for example, do you avoid sharing thoughts or feelings, asking questions, inviting him to outings, discussing questions, and sharing good or bad moments in your day? Do the good times scare you because the bad times can't be far behind?

* Can you articulate what you would miss about your partner? Are they generic things like "company" and "shared expenses" instead of personal things like "his great sense of humor"?

* Does your partner "fight dirty"? Are you afraid to try to negotiate because she has more weapons and is more willing to use them against you? Does it seem that your partner is more for herself than for the partnership?

The Security Factor

People who value the security of being in a relationship more than the relationship itself may:

* Feel weak and helpless

* Wait for their partner to leave first

* Feel that there is no way out

* Feel they can't live without their spouse

* Feel afraid of the future and paralyzed

* Feel afraid of the disapproval of others

* Use excuses and dodges to stay in their partnership (e.g., "I'm the only one who can make her happy")

* Have decided to get out before, but backed down at the BP's uses of fear, obligation, and guilt

Staying in a relationship with a BP for security is pointless. People with BPD are emotionally unstable, and looking to them for stability is hopeless. Think about what you're already providing for yourself in this relationship. What exactly is it that you would be giving up? And is there another way to get it? Write your answers in the blank space provided here.

_____

_____

_____

_____

📖 Action Step 43:
Avoiding Making a Decision

Someone once said, "Not to decide is to decide." Sometimes not making a decision about your situation is, in fact, making a decision. The following are reasons that some people give for waiting and waiting. If any of them feels familiar, mark them and write down your thoughts in your notebook.

____ **"Hey, I've got kids!"** Lots of non-BPs do. Yet this hasn't stopped them from going after what they want. It's true that in some courtrooms, custody laws and tradition favor the mother assuming custody. However, some men use this fact as an excuse to avoid making a tough choice. How do we know this? They complain they won't get custody or joint custody even though:

* They have no idea what the laws are in their state or how the process goes. Rather than read a book, they rely on hearsay and believe the worst-case scenarios.

* They have never seen a lawyer, or they have been scared off by one pessimistic lawyer.

* They have never spoken to anyone from a fathers' or children's rights' organization to learn how to obtain what they want.

* They let themselves believe that the effect of divorce on children is worse than the effect of living in an abusive environment.

____ **"I'm waiting for my partner to get better."** If your partner is in therapy and the two of you are both finding new ways to communicate, this makes sense. But if your partner is in denial, seeing a therapist only to please you or keep the status quo, or actively making your life miserable, you have not yet accepted the fact that this is as good as it gets. Is this good enough? Good enough for the rest of your life? Good enough for your children?

____ **"I don't want to be alone!"** This is a very common fear perpetuated in part by our society, where twosomes rule. If this is your fear, ask yourself how much company and friendship you're getting from your partner *now*. Take stock of your friends and family and take note of who will support you if you decide to leave. Write down in your journal what you will *gain* from being alone: no more rages, criticisms, blaming, or trying to please someone who won't be pleased, etc. You took care of your emotional needs for years before you met this person. You can do it again. Make a list of the things you would enjoy more if the BP were not in your life.

____ **"I wouldn't leave if she had cancer. Why would I leave if she had BPD?"** This analogy is *not* accurate. If your partner had cancer, she would be getting treatment. Many high-functioning BPs don't. Cancer isn't contagious. BPD thinking and behavior is. Someone with cancer doesn't manage their feelings by continually taking them out on others. Someone with BPD may. Partners work together to fight cancer and support each other. Most non-BPs with high-functioning BP partners have all the blame laid on them and are treated *like* a cancer. If your BP partner is working at treatment, then the analogy makes more sense. If she's not, it doesn't.

_____ **"No one else would want me."** This is a sure sign you need to leave this relationship now.

What about Therapy?

Many people try individual or couples marital therapy. The success of these therapies depends on the skills of the therapist, the BP's and your willingness to look at hard issues and change, the specific problems that exist, the traits of the person with BPD, and your own baggage.

If your partner is convinced that everyone else has a problem—not him—beware. The combination of this and a bad therapist can be deadly in a divorce trial.

Trust your intuition. This applies to both marital and individual counseling. Does the clinician seem to *get it*? Have years gone by without real progress? Does your partner seem to be using therapy as a false move toward progress? Have either of you gained any insight? (Your children, if you have them, might need therapy as well; there is much information about children and therapy on the Internet.)

In my opinion, the best clinicians strike a balance between exploring the past (childhood, relationships with parents, etc.) and modifying behaviors that must change *now*. For example, if you overeat in response to your situation, you can work on a substitute even as you explore your situation on a deeper level. If your partner rages, the clinician can help you set boundaries even before the disorder itself is addressed.

Remember, many people with BPD have a good response to medication. If your partner is willing, make an appointment with a psychiatrist experienced in treating BPD (see chapter 11).

If You Decide to Leave

If you decide to discontinue this relationship, I strongly recommend that you obtain the booklet *Love and Loathing: Protecting Your Mental Health and Legal Rights When Your Partner Has Borderline Personality Disorder*, described in appendix A. If you have children and you are concerned about seeing them or about their welfare in the BP's custody, the CD set *You're My World: A Non-BP's Guide to Custody* will be indispensable (see appendix A). These two items will explain what to do if your ex-partner harasses you physically or legally; help you understand why you chose the relationship; help you gain custody or maintain a relationship with your children; help you choose an experienced attorney; and help you save thousands of dollars in the process.

When the BP's Abandonment Fears Kick In

If you leave the relationship, there is a very good chance that the BP's abandonment fears will kick in and he will try to pull you back into the relationship by any means possible. This ranges from promises of change and declarations of love to threats: "You'll never see the children again!" This behavior pattern is so common that Internet support group members have named it "Hoovering" because it feels like you're getting "sucked" back in as by a vacuum cleaner.

Most BPs in this situation very sincerely believe they can change overnight. Unfortunately, their promises are not only unrealistic (people don't change their personality overnight) but originate from intolerable feelings of intense pain and loss. The good intentions don't last long, and if you give in, only one thing will be different: the BP will know you can be manipulated with promises of action—not real action.

Being "Hoovered" is a bit like hungrily biting into a sandwich, only to find it's made out of plastic. But most non-BPs are so eager for the BP to change they willingly eat the plastic and pretend it's duck à l'orange from a fancy French restaurant. If you don't watch out, you and the BP will be caught in an endless loop of forgiveness, a buildup of blame and criticism, you threatening to leave and being Hoovered back into the relationship. Some non-BPs spend years in this cycle.

📖 Action Step 44:
Turn Off That Great Sucking Sound

Helen S., a non-BP on the Internet, posted these ideas for combating being Hoovered, or being sucked back in. Check off the ideas that appeal to you and use your notebook to plan what you will do when you've left the relationship but your partner is trying to get you back.

_____ *Journal, journal, journal. Start right now and document everything you can remember that ever really hurt you in the course of the relationship: phrases used to malign you, irrational arguments, infidelities, embarrassing rages in public, pathological jealousies, verbal, physical, and emotional abuse.*

_____ *After each failed attempt to "make your opinion known" that is met with anger and rejection by your BP, write down your point of view. Then imagine what it would be like to be with a partner who could really hear it and respect it.*

_____ *Hang out with "normal" people (using "normal" very loosely): good friends, family (if this applies), colleagues, and anyone with whom you can have good, deep, honest conversations. Then contrast any of those conversations to your most recent attempt at an in-depth conversation with your BP.*

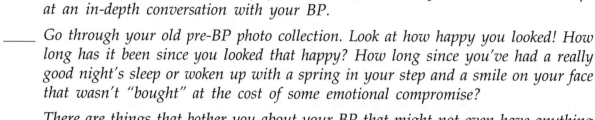

_____ *Go through your old pre-BP photo collection. Look at how happy you looked! How long has it been since you looked that happy? How long since you've had a really good night's sleep or woken up with a spring in your step and a smile on your face that wasn't "bought" at the cost of some emotional compromise?*

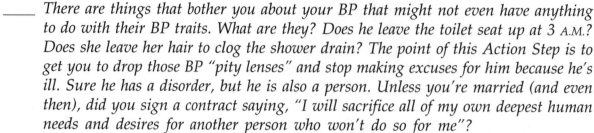

_____ *There are things that bother you about your BP that might not even have anything to do with their BP traits. What are they? Does he leave the toilet seat up at 3 A.M.? Does she leave her hair to clog the shower drain? The point of this Action Step is to get you to drop those BP "pity lenses" and stop making excuses for him because he's ill. Sure he has a disorder, but he is also a person. Unless you're married (and even then), did you sign a contract saying, "I will sacrifice all of my own deepest human needs and desires for another person who won't do so for me"?*

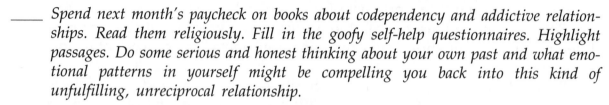

_____ *Spend next month's paycheck on books about codependency and addictive relationships. Read them religiously. Fill in the goofy self-help questionnaires. Highlight passages. Do some serious and honest thinking about your own past and what emotional patterns in yourself might be compelling you back into this kind of unfulfilling, unreciprocal relationship.*

Like many Action Steps, this one involves changing your thinking, evaluating your values, and questioning your assumptions. Getting rid of the sticky cobwebs in your head takes time, effort, and the right tools. Before you go back to this relationship, wait for your BP to enter therapy and learn to treat you in the way you want to be treated. Not falling for his Hoovering techniques may be the motivation he needs to do just that.

If the BP Is Your Child

If the BP is your minor child, one of the most difficult decisions that you may need to make is whether to put your child in a hospital or residential treatment center. If you talk to other parents, you'll probably hear a mixture of results, ranging from horror stories to hymns of praise for a life turned around. Such a range of responses can make it even harder to decide what's best for you and your child.

What can you do to make the best decision? Plan ahead and educate yourself. If your child is in crisis and you know what resources are available, you have a greater chance of making a good choice. You'll be much less emotional and more effective at researching your options if your child doesn't need them—yet.

Hospitalization

Your child's psychiatrist, if he has one, will have admitting privileges to one or more hospitals. Some may be psychiatric facilities; some may be general hospitals with a psychiatric floor or department. Interview the psychiatrist about why he might recommend one over the other. You should also get in touch with your insurance company to find out about coverage.

People often think of a psychiatric hospital as a forbidding place surrounded by tall iron fences, where society is protected from dangerous, mentally unbalanced people. The truth is that hospitals are often a place to keep patients, especially patients with BPD, safe from themselves.

Hospitalization for children with BPD is somewhat controversial. Some experts feel that patients with BPD can become too dependent on the structured world of the hospital, so such visits should be kept to a minimum. Other experts feel that a hospital or residential program can help the borderline patient understand her illness and develop strategies to cope with it.

Before exploring the world of hospitalization, you need to understand the different possibilities.

Short-term hospitalization. Sometimes called "acute care." This type of inpatient admission generally lasts for two to seven days. It can occur in a regular hospital that has a psychiatric unit or in a psychiatric hospital that handles mental illness. For the most part, this type of admission is considered crisis intervention or crisis stabilization. It isn't intended for long-term therapy.

This is an answer for what to do with children who are threatening suicide, have been seriously cutting themselves, or who are otherwise medically unstable. "They are at such a risk that they need a great deal of skilled supervision and crisis intervention," says Paul Mason, M.S., and the manager of Child and Adolescent Services at All Saints Health Care System in Racine, Wisconsin. "They may also need crisis intervention services with their whole family." These days, a week is considered a long stay for short-term hospitalization.

Long-term hospitalization in a state hospital. Here, children can stay for months to years. "That gives the staff a little bit more time to work with families and children," Mason says. "But because state hospitals are often few and sparsely located, it can be hard to work with a family because they may have a very long drive. Also, in many cases the person's behavior has to have become so problematic and pervasive that state or county human services departments have gotten involved."

Long-term hospitalization in a private psychiatric facility. These are private for-profit hospitals. Often clients of these hospitals are people with enough resources to stay for extended periods of time, as long as payment can be made. Many people believe that the best treatment is available in private facilities and the worst at state hospitals. "I disagree with that," Mason says. "The private facilities may be very comfortable, even plush, but the staff may be no better qualified than those at the state hospital. Actually, many state hospitals are training grounds for universities, and they are usually staffed by very qualified professionals." Mason emphasizes the importance of researching your options in order to make the best choice.

📖 *Action Step 45:*
Researching Treatment Centers

Most hospitals or treatment centers will work toward the following goals: Check off the ones that are appropriate for your situation.

_____ Protect the patient from self-inflicted dangers and help her avoid other high-risk situations

_____ Encourage the patient to accept his illness and begin working toward successful therapy

_____ Evaluate and revise existing outpatient therapy and tailor it to the patient's needs

_____ Provide a break for the patient and her family from each other

_____ Help a patient out of a psychotic episode

_____ Interrupt a pattern of negative reactions to outpatient therapy

_____ Address uncontrolled emotional reactions

_____ Address self-destructive, impulsive behavior

Residential Treatment Centers

"I know how hard it is to admit your child to a residential setting, but I also know that it's a lifesaver," says one mother whose daughter was so hard to handle that her parents had to hire a professional to take her to the center they had chosen. "She was violent and a huge runaway risk," this mom continues, "but the center saved her life, literally."

"Leaving my daughter in tears with a stranger in a strange town in a strange room was heartrending," says another mom. "It was a picture I will hold with me for life." And yet, looking back years later, this mother says it was the best move they ever made for their daughter.

A Residential Treatment Center (RTC), group home, or other transitional program offers longer-term care in a facility for children who need closer supervision and a more regimented program than most parents can provide. While hospitals are staffed by registered nurses, psychologists, psychiatric social workers, and psychiatrists, the staff in residential treatment facilities include a larger number and variety of non-degreed human service workers who have been trained to work with troubled children and teenagers. This type of facility should have a nurse on staff and a medical doctor who supervises. A consulting psychiatrist may visit periodically to supervise and prescribe medications.

All such programs must be licensed through the state, but they may be licensed as a group home rather than a psychiatric facility. Their focus is not on acute care or stabilization but on long-term, less intense care. Residential facilities usually provide educational services. They may hire their own teachers or work through the local public school system.

The quality of residential homes varies widely. If you are considering this option, make sure the people at the residential facility have experience with and knowledge about children with BPD. Most insurance companies won't pay for residential treatment, which can cost three to five thousand dollars a month. However, financial assistance may be available from your county or state.

To get financial assistance, you will probably need to fill out a CHINS petition (Child in Need of Services), available from your county. This is a serious step, but it gives you more options. While most parents do not want to go this far, it may allow you access to some counseling services, referrals for indicated services, and other activities to support families. It also leaves a paper trail showing that your child has a troubled history. Should your child ever make false accusations of abuse, this trail can be invaluable. Include violent outbursts, calls to the police, and reactions to medications when you do the paperwork.

📖 Action Step 46:
Rate These Residential Settings

The quality of residential facilities varies a great deal. The California Psychiatric Association recommends that you look for a facility with the following attributes. As you look at different facilities, use the checklist below to evaluate them. Keep a record in your notebook of how each facility fares in your examination of each attribute. You can grade the facility an "A" (for excellent) down to an "F" (for failing).

_____ Does every child in the residential treatment setting get an exhaustive written psychiatric evaluation when he is admitted?

_____ Is the consulting psychiatrist in communication with the treatment staff?

_____ Does the psychiatrist have easy access to people responsible for the administration, planning, and clinical operations of the treatment center?

_____ Are children on psychiatric medication seen as often as necessary to determine effectiveness, monitor side effects, and adjust dosage levels?

_____ Are children seen as frequently as necessary according to the medical judgment of the psychiatrist?

_____ Each time the child is seen by the child psychiatrist, does she chart treatment responses, patient compliance, drug side effects, and test results?

Choosing a Long-Term Program

Often parents don't have much choice about acute hospitalization. In a crisis they go to the nearest hospital with a psychiatric unit. But once the child is stabilized and you are considering a longer-term placement, you need to do a great deal of homework. Here are some suggestions. If your child is a BP and you are considering longer-term care, do the following Action Step. Check off the actions you plan to take. Many of these suggestions were given by parents of borderline children.

📖 Action Step 47:
Evaluating a Long-Term Program

_____ Start looking for a facility; don't wait until your child is ready to be discharged from the acute care unit.

_____ Visit, tour, and meet with the staff of any facility you are considering. Go at various times, day and night, and visit unannounced.

_____ Find out everything you can about the staff: their education, their training, and what types of in-service training the facility requires.

_____ Find out if this particular facility has any experience in dealing with children with BPD. If it doesn't, be leery.

_____ Ask therapists or hospital staff for their insights and recommendations.

_____ Find out treatment approaches and philosophy; conduct an in-depth interview with the director or medical staff. In particular, ask, "What will happen if my child does the very behavior they were sent in for?"

_____ Ask if the facility is willing for the child's outside psychiatrist or psychologist to continue seeing the child.

_____ Ask if there are parents of former patients who'd be willing to talk to you about their experience.

_____ Check the local paper to see how many openings the facility has. If there are a lot, find out why.

_____ Be aware that many of these facilities deal especially with young people who are multiple offenders and are in the juvenile justice system. A program designed for these children may be all wrong for a child with BPD.

_____ In the case of foster care, check out how many hours of training the foster parents have received and how much in-service training they are required to do each year. Find out if they've ever worked with children with BPD.

If Your Teen Refuses Treatment

Every state has an age of consent, usually between fourteen and sixteen, when a child can choose whether or not to be hospitalized. If a child over that age absolutely refuses to enter a hospital or treatment facility, parents have to go the involuntary commitment route. This is not easy. The child must be an immediate danger to himself or others, which can be difficult to show. And it's emotionally traumatic for children and parents alike. As one mother on the Internet said, "Watching my child shackled and shuffling in that bright orange jumpsuit and seeing those soft child's wrists in the shiny steel handcuffs—that image remains to this day the deepest scar on my psyche."

But, as wrenching as an involuntary commitment is, parents often feel it is the right move. It's an opportunity to rest and refocus on the marriage and the rest of the family. "I feel somehow lighter each day," one father says. "I'm sleeping better knowing he's where he needs to be and that I don't have to be afraid for him—or for us."

Usually, involuntary commitment is handled through the sheriff or police department, often when the child is showing some suicidal gestures or evidence of harming herself or others. The sheriff or police officer takes the child into emergency detention; this can mean a great deal of stress and endless paperwork.

"Sometimes it backfires on the parents," Mason warns. "The judge usually has seventy-two hours to assess the child and make treatment assignments. If the judge sends the child back home, the child will be very angry with you for having called the police. But he will know your boundaries: that you will not be part of violence or abuse."

Frank Picone, L.C.S.W., coordinator of Carrier's East Mountain Youth Lodge, and Carl Salierno, director of Carrier's East Mountain Youth Services, urge parents to choose their battles. If a teen is not a harm to himself or others and is not ready for treatment, you may wish to wait.

"Many parents make the common mistake of getting into power struggles with their teens. If you do, you will lose every time, because adolescents are prepared to go down with the ship," Picone says. Instead of demanding that your child obey you, tell him what is expected and let "natural and logical" consequences result if he refuses. "Adolescents need to understand that their parents do care about them, but consequences to their behavior exist," asserts Salierno. If your teen does not complete his homework assignment, let his teacher give him a failing grade. If her poor attendance means that she must repeat the grade, let her repeat it. "You should not be more invested in your teen's life than he or she is," Picone states. "One of the greatest tasks of adolescence is to learn how to function as an adult. The ultimate teacher is life itself, with all of its rewards and consequences."

Red Flags That Suggest a Placement Isn't Working

Sometimes children get into bad situations at a hospital or treatment center. Perhaps the facility isn't very good or just isn't a good match for your child.

📖 *Action Step 48:*
Keep Tabs on the Placement

Since most children (including children with BPD) will bend the truth to benefit themselves, how do you know if a placement isn't a good one for your child? According to Mason, certain signs can point the way to an accurate reading of a bad situation. If you're worried about the placement, investigate the following potential problems:

_____ Treatment approaches that don't seem appropriate (or the treatment center isn't using any recognized methods of treatment)

_____ Rumors of physical punishment or physical mishandling of children

_____ Bruises, scratches, or other signs of physical mistreatment

_____ Lack of qualified staff members working alongside the nonprofessional staff

_____ Unreasonable restrictions on your right to visit with no good explanation as to why

_____ Overuse of medication

You can expect to hear your child say, "I hate it here; they're mean to me," especially early on in placement. You will need to follow up on any accusations of ill treatment, but you must also keep in mind that some children with BPD tend to exaggerate to get their way.

If the BP Is Your Parent

This is by far the most complex relationship and one that deserves a workbook of its own. More than with any other relationship, your parent made you who you are today; made impressions when you were a small child and had no frame of reference. Therefore, rather than try to summarize a great deal of information, I will point you in the right direction to help you decide if you want to see your borderline parent, if you want to forgive him or her, and how to stand on your own two feet as an adult and assert yourself. For further information, read the following books, both described in appendix A.

_____ *Toxic Parents: Overcoming Their Hurtful Legacy and Reclaiming Your Life* (Forward 1989), especially the checklists on how you behave with your parent, how you feel when you are with her, and your beliefs about the relationship.

_____ *Understanding the Borderline Mother: Helping Her Children Transcend the Intense, Unpredictable, and Volatile Relationship* (Lawson 2000), especially the second half.

Read these books slowly and thoroughly, jotting down revelations in your notebook as you read them. They will take you gently through the process of learning to love yourself, despite the fact that you didn't get what you needed and you weren't adequately protected by your other parent.

📖 Action Step 49:
Coping with Your Emotions

This Action Step is designed to help you with your feelings about making a decision, whatever type of relationship you have with the BP. It addresses fear of the unknown—a problem we all have.

Part 1: Choose a quiet place where you will be free of distractions for about five minutes or so. Take a deep breath, relax, and free your mind of distracting thoughts. Once you're at ease, think of your greatest fear related to the BP. What is it that your BP might do to help create the very worst day of your life? Picture the whole scenario, in detail, in your mind's eye. Notice the feelings it brings. Notice any sounds, sights, or even smells that come up in the mental picture. Hold that picture for a few minutes.

Once you have clearly constructed and fixed that picture in your mind, bring yourself back into the here and now. Yawn and stretch if that helps.

Part 2: Now is the time to put your thinking hat back on. Take your notebook and describe in words the mental picture you just created. Realistically, what parts of the imaginary scene that you just created are really likely to occur? Make a list of these elements.

Below this list, make another list of the scenes that probably won't happen.

Looking at both lists, which events seem to have been created purely out of fear rather than from experience? Write them down. Now you should have three lists: the realistic events, the unrealistic events, and the events that originate from your fears. Compare and contrast the three lists.

Sometimes the logical side of our brain does not work in close harmony with the imaginative side. That can happen, for instance, if we do not acknowledge our fears. As a consequence, our fears can become like childhood monsters in the closet—never seen, but always growing in size and ferocity.

If you take the time to deliberately view something from both the logical *and* the imaginative side of your brain, then you put those two sides of yourself in dialogue with each other and they have a better opportunity to "work things out." In other words, the logical side of your brain has a better chance of filtering out the frightening "boogy men" fears.

📖 *Action Step 50:*
Making Decisions to Act Differently

This exercise will help you see your own situation by taking you into an imaginary setting that may remind you of your own life. Tape the following script in your own voice, and play it back while doing the exercise.

Part 1: Choose a time and place so you are not likely to be interrupted for ten to fifteen minutes. Take a pen or pencil and your notebook. When you are ready to begin, take a deep breath and relax.

Imagine that you are locked inside a dungeon beneath a castle. It is dark. You can see and smell the dampness on the cold gray granite walls. The air smells moldy. You are not even completely certain why you are there, but you know for sure that you must have greatly offended some very powerful person. You are frightened and very thirsty. You touch the heavy wooden door that is locked at the end of your little cell. As you do, you hear faint, eerie, but terrifying sounds of someone in the distance screaming as if in great pain, or possibly going mad from isolation. You wonder if the same fate will befall you and you begin to feel the icy grip of fear in your stomach.

Suddenly you hear the faint sound of footsteps. They are getting louder. You begin to see light through a slit in the wooden door. The steps get louder until they stop right in front of your door. You hear the sound of jingling, and you hear the scrape of an old iron key in the rusty lock.

The lock turns, and the ancient door loudly creaks open to reveal a tall, kind-faced young man who is carrying a lantern and wearing a heavy black cape held together in front with a golden brooch. He says nothing, but he smiles in a kind and encouraging way and motions for you to follow him. You feel afraid, but you are also afraid of refusing him, so you step outside the door into the light of his lantern. He turns and walks confidently down a stone hallway. You feel stiff from sitting on the cold stone floor for so long, but you push yourself to keep up with him. He recognizes that you are having some difficulty, so he turns and waits for you.

He turns down a dim hallway to the left, then another to the right, then up a flight of stone stairs, and then up another flight. You begin to feel the air grow lighter and cleaner as you ascend. You feel grateful to this stranger, but you still don't know what is happening. You wonder for a moment if he is taking you to the executioner, but you quickly try to push that idea out of your thoughts. Soon you are standing at an iron gate, and on the other side of the gate you see sunshine and green grass. The stranger turns and smiles gently once more before taking out a large brass key and working it into a keyhole in the gate. With a bit of effort, he turns the lock and opens the iron gate. Then he smiles at you one last time and says, "You are free. You may go."

You hear the sounds of a water fountain splashing somewhere beyond the gate, and you're reminded of your great thirst. You desperately want to go outside in the warm sun and the cool grass, but you still feel afraid. Unsure of yourself, you turn to the stranger and ask, "But who locked me in that dungeon cell? And why? Am I still in trouble? What if they come after me again? What can I do then? And who are you? Why are you letting me go free now?" In answer, he turns and looks directly at you, eyes warm, compassionate, and steady. He simply repeats himself: "You may go now. You are free."

Confused, but glad to be in a nicer place, you step outside into the warm sunshine. You feel the sun on your clothes, your hair, your arms, your face. You turn toward where you heard the water splashing, and you see a large fountain with a large white statue standing in the middle of the pool. People are quietly and peacefully standing by the fountain filling their cups and pitchers, but all gathering the clear cool water. Some are filling their hands and drinking right where they stand, while others are carrying away full pitchers. You walk toward the fountain. You cannot help but think about how you feel. Only moments ago, you were lost, confined, helpless, and confused. Now, you are still uncertain as to what lies ahead for you, but at least your are warm, comfortable, and free. You think about the contrast between where you were a short while ago and where you are now. There is still something strange, something unexplained, about the whole story.

You turn these events over and over in your mind, and you keep thinking about the last thing the young stranger said to you: "You may go now. You are free." That was the turning point for you. What if you had not stepped outside? What if you had been too afraid? Would he have locked the iron gate again? A curious mixture of feelings flows through you as you ponder these questions. Someone hands you a ceramic cup that just fits your hand, and says, "Drink! There's plenty of water here."

Part 2: Now it is time to bring your attention back to the here and now. Take a slow deep breath and release it. Now slowly look around and notice where you are and what is around you. Notice the sounds, sights, and smells in your immediate environment. Now it is time to put your thinking hat back on again. Think back on how you felt at each stage of the story as it unfolded. How did you feel being alone in the dungeon cell? In your notebook, describe the feeling as best you can. Do you ever feel that way in real life? When? Under what circumstances? If so, write down when, where, and under what circumstances you have felt that way before. How have you felt when you realized that someone else was suffering, probably more than you were?

As the story unfolded, how did you feel when you heard someone coming toward your cell? When they opened the door? When they invited you to step outside? Are any of those feelings familiar? Write down the answer to each of these questions as well. Most importantly, how did you feel as you stood on the threshold of freedom? Take some time and put those feelings into words, writing them down.

As human beings, we are creatures of habit. We get comfortable in our ruts, whatever they are, because adapting to our environment is a built-in survival mechanism. However, there are times and places when being comfortable with our habits and our circumstances can work against us.

In those situations, we can become habituated to things that have destructive effects on us. Whenever that happens, we can get into a condition that has been called "learned helplessness." This simply means that, consciously or unconsciously, we somehow recognize our situation as being one in which our chances of survival are better if we just lie low and don't do anything to draw attention to ourselves. When we reach this stage, we may become fearful of asserting ourselves, fearful of taking control of our circumstances, fearful of acting on our own behalf.

There is something about the nature of BPD that it often seems to have a long-term cumulative effect on family members. Remember, the BP is seeking inner stability, emotional stability, and a BP who has not been educated about the disease process naturally tends to try to find stability by controlling people around him.

Your mission, should you choose to accept it, is to gain an understanding of the fact that your BP's misinformed and misguided efforts to control her emotions by controlling *your* actions does not help anyone, and therefore there is no reason for you to support her efforts. It may be unfamiliar, uncomfortable, even frightening, but you *can* take control of your life again.

Each type of relationship has its own set of criteria. In brief, if the BP is someone with whom you must have a relationship in order to have another, more important relationship, it is important to be supported, stay detached, use nondefensive communication, and refuse to be drawn into battle. An example of this would be a relationship with a daughter-in-law. Remember that the BP sees you as a threat; your goal is to show her that people have an infinite capacity for love.

If the BP is someone you expect to fill your needs, your challenge is to look at the situation the way it is—not the way it was or the way you would like it to be—and to give yourself permission to have your own needs. Your decisions must be based on reality, not fantasy.

If the BP is an abusive person from whom you need protection (or if you need to protect others), take this job very seriously. Do not rationalize any kind of verbal, emotional, physical, or sexual abuse. If children are involved, their safety comes first, whether the BP is their parent, sibling, or your child. The BP must make his or her own choices, and so must you. Make sure that your choice is the right one for the long term.

Chapter 11

Finding Qualified
Professional Help

When I try to find help for my borderline wife, some clinicians tell me there is no such thing as BPD. I'd like to say, "'Why don't you spend a week with my wife?' Then I'd like to hear what you have to say."

—a man on the Internet

*F*inding a clinician who is experienced in treating BPD is one of the most difficult issues BPs and non-BPs encounter. People ask me for recommendations several times a week.

The problem is that, in essence, the clinician must help the BP work through the anger, frozen grief, and other powerful emotions that are currently being directed your way. It takes a skilled person to set personal limits while being accessible, to help the BP like himself while motivating him to change, and to develop a close rapport without encouraging too much dependence. Clinicians are just like you in that they have triggers and personal feelings; they're just trained to deal with them.

First, Do No Harm

It can be difficult to find a clinician with BPD clients. At best, uninformed clinicians do not help. At worst, they make the situation worse, as one clinician who wishes to remain anonymous explained in an interview with me:

> *One of my principal concerns is the absence of adequate training in the recognition and treatment of BPD, which results in bad outcomes for many. Most of my current clients ended up with me after multiple prior treatment failures, often because the therapist, while well-meaning, did more harm than good. Much of the damage occurs because the therapists have lousy boundaries, either because of their own issues or because they are inadequately trained.*
>
> *The "harm" results when the therapist recognizes the boundary violations and suddenly changes the rules, even blaming the BPD patient. Since issues of trust, rejection, and safety are so important to the BPD client, this therapist behavior can be very destructive.*
>
> *The second type of harm often occurs when patients requiring long-term treatment are invited into a short-term process, only to be dropped when money runs out. BPD patients need to understand what they are undertaking, up front. Most of the other problems occur via simple therapist incompetence.*

Why Finding a Clinician Is Difficult

There are a number of reasons why it is hard to find professional help.

1. Clinicians generally do not get enough training in personality disorders. I am a layperson, yet in every clinical workshop I do, I must spend half of my time defining BPD before I can start discussing its effect on families. Clinicians who went to school before 1980 graduated at a time when BPD wasn't even a formal diagnosis in the *DSM*.

2. Clinicians shun personality-disordered patients in general. For example, in *The Minds of Billy Milligan* (Keyes 1993), psychiatrist Frederick Milkie is documented as having testified in court about his method of treating one of his patients, Billy Milligan. In response to a question from Assistant

Attorney General David Belinski as to how he treated Milligan, Milkie answered, "with skillful neglect."

3. People worldwide need help, and there is currently no international database of clinicians with expertise in treating personality disorders who are taking patients.

4. A clinician who may work well with one person may not develop rapport with another. No credential or recommendation can guarantee a clinician's ability to help you or those you love.

5. People with BPD are some of the most difficult people to treat. Reiland (2002) describes beings so angry at her psychiatrist that she threatened a false sexual harassment complaint and once left a semi-threatening note on her psychiatrist's car. Two clinicians have personally told me of BPs who self-harmed during a counseling session and needed immediate medical treatment. Yet, many clinicians find BPs some of the most rewarding people to treat; although therapy with BPs takes longer and is more difficult, the successes are all the more gratifying.

6. Universities do not emphasize personality disorders, and a clinician may get just a few hours of training on BPD. Faculty members do not necessarily keep up with the latest research and have been known to discourage their students from accepting borderline clients.

7. Potential patients do not always feel comfortable hiring a clinician in the same way they might select a painter for their home. James Paul Shirley explains that people should not feel embarrassed to ask tough questions.

8. There is no clear agreement on the best medication and therapy for people with BPD, although this is an area of active research. We still don't know the cause of the disorder, which makes it nearly impossible to agree on a therapy. Thus far dialectical behavior therapy (DBT), a cognitive behavioral therapy developed by Marsha Linehan, Ph.D., seems most effective. DBT emphasizes teaching patients practical skills, providing support, and balancing self-acceptance with the need for change.

There are two kinds of issues in a therapeutic relationship: contractual issues and therapeutic issues. Contractual issues include things like appointment schedules, professional fees, and whether or not a given clinician has anything to offer you in resolving your problems. Therapeutic issues are those issues you talk about once the contractual issues are settled—your thoughts, feelings, actions, life circumstances, relationships, etc. Any worthwhile clinician will be very glad to hear you express your uneasy feelings about the therapeutic relationship. If they treat those uneasy feelings as though they represent something "wrong" with you, though, don't waste any more time on that clinician. Do not pass "Go" and do not collect $200—cut a trail right then, and look for another therapist. I know one individual who experienced exactly that sort of unease with a therapist, feeling vaguely that something was wrong but unable to put his finger on it, and later through his own research he discovered that the "professional" was not even licensed to practice.

Dialectical Behavior Therapy

DBT is also the only therapy that has treatment standards that stay the same from clinician to clinician. You can do a search on dialectical behavior therapy on BPDCentral (www.BPDCentral.com) or on the Internet. There are also books on the subject. The Behavioral Technology Transfer Group, Linehan's training organization, is in the process of posting an updated list of clinicians who have been through dialectical behavior therapy (DBT) training. Please refer to the Web site's clinical resource directory at: http://behavioraltech.com or, if you would like information on a DBT-trained clinician in a specific location and cannot find it on the site, phone the office at 206-675-8588, or e-mail the group at information@ behavioraltech.com. Another place to find a DBT-trained therapist is http:// brtc.psych.washington.edu (click on "Clinical Services").

Many clinicians, including those trained in DBT, are more familiar with treating low-functioning BPs who self-harm or have substance abuse or eating disorders. When interviewing clinicians, make sure they understand that Oz is also populated by high-functioning BPs who do not fit their stereotype of what a borderline patient is like.

A Method for Finding a Clinician in Any Town

Not every clinician has to be DBT-trained to be right for you. Finding the right clinician can take a lot of time and effort. But depending on your insurance plan—you might be spending a great deal of money on this—you should at least give it the same amount of research that you would a new car. More importantly, the wrong clinician can make things worse if you or the BP trust a person who is not capable of observing limits, who does not keep up with studies about BPD, or who is fooled by the borderline's mask.

When I tried this method, I called two different hospitals and got the name of the same psychiatrist—someone whom I knew well because I interviewed him for *SWOE*.

Use the following steps to help you find a clinician in your town.

1. Start by collecting the names of two to five psychiatrists. Make a list of the hospitals in town with the best inpatient psychiatric care. If there is a teaching hospital affiliated with a university, put it on your list. Then call and ask for the nurse manager in the unit or the administrative assistant in the medical staff office. Build some rapport by being friendly, and ask if this is a good time to talk. In the same voice that you might use with a friend, say

you are looking for a psychiatrist who specializes in personality disorders (do not mention BPD in particular) and ask if there is one he or she might recommend. If there is a secondary problem such as anorexia or substance abuse, mention this as well. Call back if the nurse or staff member is busy, or leave a number if you can. These people work with the psychiatric staff every day and know their reputations.

If you are in an HMO, call the hospitals where "Dr. Smith," or one of the doctors you found, practices—but do not mention his or her name. At the end of the conversation, drop in the physician's name—"Oh, by the way, do you know if Dr. Smith see patients with personality disorders?" Listen closely. No one will be disrespectful to a member of the medical staff. But listen closely for pauses, vague responses, or other noncommittal answers. You can ask, "If you had to recommend someone to a friend, who would you recommend?" If you can make them empathize with you, they will give you a name or two. Put the names in your notebook.

2. Check to see if the recommended psychiatrists are in your insurance plan. If so, call their office and make the same inquiries to the office staff. Staff members who like working there will be enthusiastic about the clinician. Staff members who are not will be less so. Use your intuition. Make an appointment with the ones who sound the best. When you meet, describe the situation and ask the following questions (write the answers in your notebook). In general, you are looking for someone who is experienced but not jaded, someone who knows a lot but is open-minded, someone who is caring but can observe firm boundaries, someone with the patience to work with someone in the long term—and someone who has a quality of caring that shines through, despite a certain amount of necessary professionalism.

Questions to Ask Psychiatrists

_____ Do you treat people with BPD? If so, how many have you treated? (At minimum, you want someone who is experienced in treating people with personality disorders.)

_____ How do you define BPD? (Most clinicians are unaware of high-functioning BPs and the problems they cause. After all, high-functioning BPs don't seek therapy.)

_____ What do you believe causes BPD? (Make sure that you and the clinician see eye to eye on the causes of BPD. Many clinicians believe that BPD always comes from parental abuse despite research and other evidence to the contrary.)

_____ What is your treatment plan for borderline clients? (Look for a flexible plan that has specific goals and does not let the client drift from session to session.)

____ Do you believe that borderlines can get better? If so, have you personally treated BPs who improved?

____ How much do you know about the stresses of living with someone with the disorder? (You may want to recommend that the clinician read *SWOE*; many know of it, but not all have actually read it. The clinician's answer may give you a clue as to how important the subject is to him. In general, look for clinicians who work with families as well as individuals. It is essential that both you and the therapist are working in the same direction and reinforcing each other.

____ Have you ever treated a high-functioning BP?

James Paul Shirley strongly believes that people trust their instincts about the clinicians they visit.

> Trust your gut feeling. Don't make gut feelings the CEO of your life, but certainly treat them like a reliable courier bringing you some reconnaissance information.
>
> There are clinicians who are not skilled in treating BPD but fail to recognize those professional limitations, much less openly acknowledge them to their clients or their clients' families. There are also therapists who feel such a driving need to be rescuers, wanting to be knights on white horses rescuing damsels in distress, that they get inflated whenever a BP splits them good and may consequently cast you, the non-BP, as the eternal villain. Fortunately such clinicians are a minority and do not represent the profession as a whole. However, they are out there, and you should never underestimate the potential for such a clinician to create even greater harm. Use your heart, your common sense, and trust in your gut feelings. If that quiet, nagging feeling tugging at your tummy tells you something is wrong, then it probably is. If you get that uneasy feeling around a certain clinician, treat that feeling like a piece of information that needs further checking. Above all, do not ever permit a clinician to treat your concerns as "symptoms."

Step 3: Depending on your situation, you or your BP loved one should consider seeing the psychiatrist for an assessment. Some psychiatrists offer therapy as well as psychiatric evaluations.

Whether or not you do, the psychiatrist should be able to refer you to a therapist experienced with BPD.

Appendix A

Reading List
and Resources

While there are many other resources about BPD and related issues, these are the most recent, the most accurate, and the best.

For Anyone with an Interest in BPD

Organizations

Personality Disorders Awareness Network (PDAN) A non-profit organization dedicated to raising the profile of BPD, offering Internet resources and support for family members, and encouraging consumers to demand better BPD treatment. This organization maintains the www.BPDCentral.com website and the Welcome to Oz support groups. Your tax-deductible donation will help thousands of people such as yourself and may be made as follows:
By Credit Card
1. Web site: http://www.paypal.com
2. e-mail: RandiBPD@aol.com
3. Toll Free: 888-357-4355 or 800-431-1579
By Check
4. Payable to PDAN
PO Box 070106
Milwaukee, WI 53207-0106

National Education Alliance for Borderline Personality Disorder (NEA-BPD)
The NEA-BPD is a non-profit organization that focuses on families. It seeks to provide education on BPD, to dispel the myths that surround it, and to bring hope for a better life. Its goals are to disseminate information through the sponsoring of a yearly conference, to maintain a Web site that offers current information and research, and to establish regional centers for families that provide information, support, and training.
Contacts: Perry Hoffman and Dixianne Penney. Phone 914-835-9011, or e-mail: NEABPD@aol.com
Web site: www.borderlinepersonalitydisorder.com

New England Personality Disorders Association (NEPDA) McLean Hospital— Bowditch, 115 Mill Street, Belmont, Mass. 02478. Phone 617-855-2000 or 617-855-2680, or e-mail: info@NEPDA.org.
Offers information and self-help groups for families.

Books

I'm Not Supposed to Be Here: My Recovery from Borderline Personality Disorder, 2002, by Rachel Reiland, Eggshells Press. A true, first-person account of how the author overcame Borderline Personality Disorder with the support of an experienced and caring psychiatrist. A moving, original book that gives the best picture I've ever read of how it feels to have the disorder and how the disorder impacts the family. Available only from Eggshells Press at 888-357-4355 (888-35-SHELL).

Stop Walking on Eggshells: Taking Your Life Back When Someone You Care About Has Borderline Personality Disorder, 1998, by Paul Mason, M.S., and Randi Kreger, New Harbinger Publications. *SWOE* is in its seventh printing and has been purchased by people in thirty different countries. "An excellent resource for making sense of borderline madness," says one review. Available anywhere books are sold, including Eggshells Press, 888-357-4355.

Codependent No More: How to Stop Controlling Others and Start Caring for Yourself, 1996, Melody Beattie, Harper and Row. This book explains why this type of thinking will only make you unhappy and tell you how controlling your own life instead of trying to control the lives of others will bring you real happiness.

Better Boundaries: Owning and Treasuring Your Own Life, 1997, by Jan Black and Greg Enns, New Harbinger Publications. This book is different than any other books on boundaries because it assumes that people must treasure and honor themselves before they can create boundaries. It then teaches you how to be your own best friend and gives the mechanics of setting and observing personal limits. Highly recommended.

The Dance of Anger: A Woman's Guide to Changing the Patterns of Intimate Relationships, 1997, Harriet Lerner, Harper and Row. For men and women, despite the title. A groundbreaking and life-changing book for anyone who believes they would be much happier if only someone else in their life would change.

The Emotionally Abused Woman: Overcoming Destructive Patterns and Reclaiming Yourself, 1990, Beverly Engel, M.F.C.C., Fawcett Columbine. Engel highlights the problems of and solutions to emotional and verbal abuse. Since nearly every non-BP suffers from abuse, this is probably a vital book for your library.

Internet Support

BPDCentral: http://www.BPDCentral.com
My Web site contains message boards, a chat room, referrals to programs and therapists, a list of online support groups, updated links to related sites, information about Eggshells Press books and tapes, and more. Recommended by John G. Gunderson., M.D., in his new book *Borderline Personality Disorder: A Clinical Guide.* From there you can subscribe to Border-Lines, an e-mail newsletter about BPD.

Helen's World of BPD Resources: http://home.hvc.rr.com/helenbpd/
A giant compilation of links about BPD, including support groups and sites that contain significant amounts of text and information.

Borderline Personality Disorder Research Foundation:
http://www.borderlineresearch.org
The Borderline Personality Disorder Research Foundation is an international, multidisciplinary, renowned group of scientists coordinating research at six universities to draw on each other's strengths in developing an integrated research paradigm to study BPD.

International Society for the Study of Personality Disorders: http://www.ISSPD.com
The International Society for the Study of Personality Disorders (ISSPD), stimulates and supports scholarship, clinical experience, and international collaboration and communication about research on all aspects of personality disorders, including both diagnosis, course, and treatment.

Behavioral Technology Transfer Group: http://www.behavioraltech.com
This Web site allow you to search for a clinician trained in dialectical behavior therapy, a successful method for treating people with BPD.

The WTO Internet Support Groups for Those with a BP Loved One (any relationship). Subscribe at http://www.egroups.com/community/NonBP-Main or http://www. egroups.com/community/WelcomeToOz

My Trip to Oz and Back: http://hometown.aol.com/nonbp99/home.html
A site that is a fifty-page letter from a non-BP to her BP partner about their relationship and why the non-BP chose to leave it. Gives a non-BP's perspective in much detail.

For People Whose Partner Has BPD

Books and CDs

Love and Loathing: Protecting Your Mental Health and Legal Rights When Your Partner Has Borderline Personality Disorder, 2000, by Kim Williams-Justesen and Randi Kreger, Eggshells Press. *Love and Loathing* helps people understand why they may have chosen a borderline partner and make a decision about whether to stay or leave the relationship. If readers choose to leave, *Love and Loathing* cautions them about the pitfalls they may encounter, helps them navigate the courts, and explains how to try to protect children from vengeful partners and an unenlightened legal system. Available from Eggshells Press at 888-357-4355 (888-35-SHELL).

If You Had Controlling Parents: How to Make Peace with Your Past and Take Your Place in This World, 1998, by Dan Neuharth, Ph.D., Cliff Street Books. This book truly excels in taking certain BPD traits and showing couples exactly what effects a BP's parenting style can have on their child. It is a wake-up call for parents who need to protect their children from parenting that is smothering, depriving, perfectionistic, chaotic, abusive, or needy.

You're My World: A Non-BP's Guide to Custody, 2001, Eggshells Press. A set of three compact discs with practical information on how to gain custody from a BP spouse if you live within the United States of America or Canada. I moderate a conversation between Ken Lewis, Ph.D., and James Paul Shirley, M.S.W. Lewis is a Registered Custody Evaluator (R.C.E.) who specializes in interstate cases. Over the past 22 years, he has been court appointed as either a custody evaluator or child advocate in 29 states and Canada. He is the director of Child Custody Evaluation Services of Philadelphia, Inc. Available from Eggshells Press at 888-357-4355 (888-35-SHELL).

Internet Support

Internet support groups for partners who wish to stay with their borderline loved one:
   http://www.egroups.com/community/WTOStaying
   http://www.egroups.com/community/NonBP-Staying

For gay and lesbian people with a BP partner who only want to be with other GLBT members:
   http://www.egroups.com/community/WTOGLBT
   http://www.egroups.com/community/nonBP-GLBT

Internet support groups for those ambivalent about staying with or leaving their BP:
   http://www.egroups.com/community/WTOtransitions
   http://www.egroups.com/community/NonBP-transitions

Internet support groups for people who want to be with those who are divorcing and are seeking legal help and support:
   http://www.egroups.com/community/WTODivorcing
   http://www.egroups.com/community/NonBP-Divorcing

Internet support groups for people who are co-parenting with a BP:
   http://www.egroups.com/community/WTOparenting
   http://www.egroups.com/community/nonBP-parenting

For People Whose Son or Daughter Has BPD

Hope for Parents: Helping Your Borderline Son or Daughter Without Sacrificing Your Family or Yourself, 2000, by Kathy Winkler and Randi Kreger, Eggshells Press. Drawing on the experiences of 250 parents whose children were diagnosed with BPD, this booklet helps parents of both adult and minor children who have BPD. It offers suggestions for finding treatment, working with care providers, countering false accusations of abuse, handling crises, fostering independence, handling finances, protecting siblings, and maintaining hope. Available from Eggshells Press at 888-357-4355 (888-35-SHELL).

Internet Support

An Internet support group for non-BPs with borderline offspring of any age: http://groups.yahoo.com/group/WTOParentsOfBPs.

An Internet support group for non-BPs who are concerned about their grandchildren:
http://groups.yahoo.com/group/WTOPgrandparents.

For People with a Borderline Parent

Understanding the Borderline Mother: Helping Her Children Transcend the Intense, Unpredictable, and Volatile Relationship, 2000, by Christine Lawson, Jason Aronson, Inc. This book is easy to read and packed with information that you need to know if you had a mother with BPD traits. Lawson breaks down BPs into four types. Adult children will probably find that their parent leans toward one of these types, but will probably see elements of the three other types in their parent. People interested in this book may also be interested in books for those with mothers who have Narcissistic Personality Disorder. These include *Trapped in the Mirror* by Elan Golomb (William Morrow and Company) and *Children of the Self-Absorbed* by Nina W. Brown (New Harbinger Publications). A must-have for anyone coping with BPD behavior. Available anywhere books are sold.

Toxic Parents: Overcoming Their Hurtful Legacy and Reclaiming Your Life, 1989, by Susan Forward, Ph.D., Bantam Books. Although it deals with all kinds of dysfunctional parents, this book is a must-have for anyone with a borderline parent.

ModOasis: http://groups.yahoo.com/group/ModOasis
An Internet support group for non-BPs with one borderline parent (mostly mothers).

Internet Support Groups

For people who prefer a Christian environment:
http://www.egroups.com/community/WTOChristian
http://www.egroups.com/community/NonBP-christian

For those dealing with BPs at work:
http://www.egroups.com/community/WTOatwork
http://www.egroups.com/community/nonBP-atwork